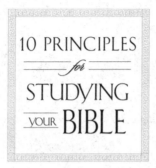

10 PRINCIPLES

for

STUDYING

YOUR **BIBLE**

Other Books by Charles Stanley

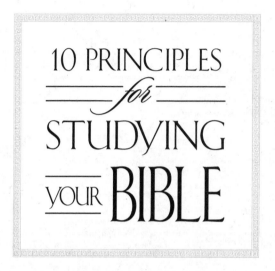

10 PRINCIPLES *for* STUDYING *your* BIBLE

CHARLES F. STANLEY

THOMAS NELSON
Since 1798

NASHVILLE DALLAS MEXICO CITY RIO DE JANEIRO

Published in Nashville, Tennessee, by Thomas Nelson. Thomas Nelson is a registered trademark of Thomas Nelson, Inc.

Thomas Nelson, Inc., titles may be purchased in bulk for educational, business, fund-raising, or sales promotional use. For information, please e-mail SpecialMarkets@ThomasNelson.com.

Unless otherwise noted, Scripture quotations are taken from the NEW AMERICAN STANDARD BIBLE®. © The Lockman Foundation 1960, 1962, 1963, 1968, 1971, 1972, 1973, 1975, 1977, 1995. Used by permission.

Scripture quotations marked NIV are from the HOLY BIBLE: NEW INTERNATION-AL VERSION®. © 1973, 1978, 1984 by International Bible Society. Used by permission of Zondervan. All rights reserved.

Library of Congress Cataloging-in-Publication Data

Stanley, Charles F.
    10 principles for studying your Bible / by Charles Stanley.
       p. cm.
    Summary: "10 Principles for Studying the Bible teaches readers the ten most essential aspects of a rich, personal encounter with God through His Word"—Provided by publisher.
    ISBN: 978-1-4002-0097-9 (tradepaper)
    1. Bible—Study and teaching. I. Title. II. Title: Ten principles for studying your Bible.
BS600.3.S73 2008
220.071—dc22

                         2007041009

Printed in the United States of America
20 21 22 LSCH 30 29 28 27

This book of the law shall not depart from your mouth,
but you shall meditate on it day and night,
so that you may be careful to do according to all
that is written in it;
for then you will make your way prosperous,
and then you will have success.

Joshua 1:8

CONTENTS

BUILT ON THE ROCK

When the rain stopped and the sun reemerged, the family returned home to survey the damage. It was all destroyed—everything from the front porch to the garage out back. The house had been built too close to the beach, and there was no way it could remain standing after taking a direct hit from a powerful hurricane, but that had not been a consideration months earlier during the home's construction. On September 15, 1999, Hurricane Floyd trained its eye on North Carolina's coast and in particular, its barrier islands. At first, weather forecasters downplayed the storm's power saying it had lost strength and was only a category two.

Days earlier, this same coastline had been pounded by Hurricane Dennis that packed torrential rains and seventy-mile-per-hour winds. Ten days later, Hurricane Floyd delivered a final blow to many of the homes in its path. Up to the last moment, experts had continued to report that there was nothing to be concerned about except additional heavy rain and moderate flooding. But their estimate was wrong. In fact, it was dead wrong. After it left Florida, Floyd regained some of its original strength while crossing over the warm waters of the Atlantic Ocean. When it made landfall in North Carolina, it was a major category three storm and caused major flooding, loss of life, and miles of destruction that stretched inland. Homes on the barrier island were leveled to the point of being unrecognizable. It was the worst natural disaster in North Carolina's history. Two and a half months earlier—in mid-June—with the sun beaming down on the vacationers, no one saw this coming. I want to use this example to underscore a very important lesson that we find in Scripture. It is one that Jesus taught His disciples, and I believe it is crucial to living a successful Christian life.

"Therefore everyone who hears these words of Mine and acts on them, may be compared to a wise man who built his house on the rock. And the rain fell, and the floods came, and the winds blew and slammed against the house; and yet it did not fall, for it had been founded on the rock. Everyone who hears these words of Mine and does not act on them, will be like a foolish man who built his house on the sand. The rain fell, and the floods came, and the winds blew and slammed against that house; and it fell—and great was its fall."

> When Jesus had finished these words, the crowds were
> amazed at His teaching; for He was teaching them as one
> having authority, and not as their scribes. (Matt. 7:24–29)

The disciples understood the story but needed help with the lesson of the parable. Weather changes in the region were not uncommon. Palestine was known to experience sudden strong storms. Rains could be so fierce that dusty, dry gullies would become torrents sweeping away anything in their path.

The example of two people building houses on different locations is perfect for what we are about to study. The man who built his house on the sand saw it fall in destruction. No matter how great the construction, the foundation was not built on solid ground. It was constructed on sand—something that can erode quickly when the storms of life come. Another man built his house on a rock foundation. Therefore, when the rain beat hard against it, it withstood the pressure. When a cruel and intense wind began to blow, it was not shaken. And when the flood-waters rose, it was not washed away because its foundation was anchored to the rock.

There is no question about which foundation is stronger. When we build our lives on the truth of God's Word, we are building on an eternal foundation that cannot be destroyed. We are building on the Rock—the Lord Jesus Christ. Those who have never given their lives to Him are living on a sandy shoreline—one that is sure to wash away. While physical storms may not always inflict great pain or suffering, emotional and mental storms do. However, you do not have to go through life wondering if the next storm will be the one that washes your life out to sea. God has an answer for your greatest need, and it is found in the study of His Word. This is your sure foundation. As you open the Bible, ask Him to reveal Himself to you and then to teach you more about His love every day. Your life will be changed, and you will be blessed far beyond what you can imagine because you have built your life on an unshakable foundation—the Lord Jesus Christ.

CHAPTER 1

COME!

Moses lifted his eyes and saw the flames in the distance. Something was burning on the side of the mountain—something unlike anything he had ever seen. He watched it—at first with curiosity, but then with wonder. It was a consuming fire. Yet the bush that contained the flame was not destroyed. For years, he had shepherded his father-in-law's flocks and on occasion noticed fires burning in the distance, but this one was different. It was more than a campfire of a neighboring shepherd. This fire burned with intensity and contained no hint of going out. Moses stood and watched this sight. Maybe he continued to move the flock from one place to another, noting that the fire was just as powerful in the evening as it had been in the first part of the day. Finally, he could wait no longer. He said, "I must turn aside now and see this marvelous sight, [and discover] why the bush is not burned up" (Exod. 3:3).

God has a divine purpose resting behind events in life.

Nothing is coincidental. The bush burned because He wanted to gain Moses' attention. He wanted Him to draw near. Sometimes His purpose for our lives is very clear. Sometimes it is not. It can appear to be very mysterious, but it never is to God. We may find ourselves asking, "God, what are You doing?" Certainly, Moses was in wonder over the sight of the burning bush. And more than likely, he wanted to know why it was not consumed.

Have you ever wondered why God allows certain challenges, events, and trials to take place? Most of us have. We encounter a serious problem and immediately are tempted to feel hopeless. Other times, when we sense a change we may actually welcome it. We find ourselves longing to have His wisdom, but how do we gain this? There is only one place, and that is in the company of God. God drew Moses to Himself. He knew exactly how His future deliverer would respond, and He knows how we will respond when He calls to us. "When the LORD saw that [Moses] turned aside to look, God called to him from the midst of the bush and said, 'Moses, Moses!' And he said, 'Here I am'" (v. 4). Forty years of living in a vast wilderness changed Moses. God had used the experience to prepare him for service. There probably was a time when he would not have noticed the flame that burned on the side of God's holy mountain. But this was no longer the case. God was drawing him close to Himself. How does He draw you and me close to Himself? Often it is in the same way, but the circumstances are different.

He may allow us to experience a challenge that is much greater than our ability to handle it. Moses spent forty years in a wilderness without the comforts that he once knew in Egypt. But each day was a day that God used to shape his life and prepare him for what he would do in the future. Each step he took was a step closer to becoming the man God created him to be.

He may set up a scenario to gain our attention. Moses saw a bush that was in full blaze, yet it was not destroyed. It definitely caught his eye, and he wondered how this could be happening. You may find yourself in a situation that is nothing like the one Moses saw unfold before him. It could be something as simple as standing in line at the grocery store and suddenly becoming aware of God's awesome love. Or you may be at home reading your morning devotional and suddenly you know God wants to speak to you about an incident or challenge that you have encountered. How do you know this? The words written on the page of your devotional book or Bible almost leap off. It is as if they are underlined and you are stopped by what you have read.

Regardless of how God draws us near, our response should be this: "Lord, I am here; speak to me and show me what You want to teach me." He may just want you to worship Him for a few minutes as you step away from the hurried pace of our world. Or He may want you to draw even closer through the study of His Word. This is where we uncover the deeper things of God— His nature, characteristics, and way. You cannot truly know God until you take time to read and study the Bible. Every question you have is answered within its pages. There is nothing you can think of that God has not thought of before you and fully explained in the text of His Word.

God loves you so much that He wants you to have His very best, but you cannot experience this outside of knowing Him. When you spend time studying His Word, you begin to realize that you are gaining the knowledge you need for a lifetime of devotion to Him. He also provides the wisdom you need for every circumstance of life. He withholds nothing. "For the LORD God is a sun and shield; the LORD gives grace and glory; no good thing does He withhold from those who walk uprightly" (Ps. 84:11). But you cannot discover God's will for your life or for the situation that you are in apart from spending time with Him. This includes studying His Word with a notepad and an open heart.

I Want to Know You, Lord

When Moses stepped into God's presence for the first time, an intimate relationship began to form between him and the Lord. At the burning bush in Exodus 3, we read that Moses "hid his face, for he was afraid to look at God" (v. 6). However, by Exodus 33, there is an entirely different account of their meetings. Verse 11 states, "The LORD used to speak to Moses face to face, just as a man speaks to his friend." Moses drew near to God and became so involved with Him that he wanted to learn His ways. And this made the difference in his life and in the relationship he had with the Lord.

Often I ask people if they study their Bibles, especially when they are seeking counsel about an issue that is very clearly outlined in God's Word. I'm always surprised at the number of times I hear, "I try, but it is too hard to understand. I just leave the preaching and the studying up to you. I try to listen on Sundays." There is nothing difficult about reading God's Word. If you are having trouble, it could be the result of something that needs to be addressed such as a lack of faith in God or some unconfessed sin.

When we doubt His Word to us, we will not have the tools we need to see the circumstances of life clearly. I've counseled people and reminded them of God's promises for a certain situation. Before I could finish my sentence, they began talking, and usually their sentence began with, "But," and then they went on to give one excuse after another as to why God would not work on their behalf. This is what I mean by a lack of faith. God's love for us is everlasting. When you turn and come to Him, He will not cast you away. Moses lived on the back side of the desert for forty years. He probably thought no one cared for him, but God did. He loved Moses with an everlasting love. This is the same love He has for you and me. Moses, however, did not have the Holy Spirit or the Word of God to guide him. He had to rely on entering into God's presence and listening for His instruction.

Without the Holy Spirit we do not have the ability to comprehend God's truth. Yet the moment we surrender our lives to Him, He pours out His truth to us in such a way that we understand all we are being taught. If there is a question, He will take as much time as needed to teach us His truth. But if we want to unlock the truths the Bible contains, we must pick it up and begin to study it. God's Spirit is willing to teach us what we need to know, but first we must make ourselves available to Him.

Through the study of God's Word, we also learn the deeper things of God. It is one thing to know He loves us, but it is entirely different to realize that He has a plan for our lives. One of Satan's greatest lies is that we can do anything we want to do and still be in the will of God. I have watched as young men and women become frustrated in their Christian walk and drift in their faith. Years ago, when I was first offered a position at First Baptist Atlanta, I remember thinking, *God is going to have to make His will crystal clear.* I was the senior pastor in Bartow, Florida. If I took the position in Atlanta, I would be an associate pastor. It did not make sense to me, but I also realized that many times God's plan is not something we can understand from a human perspective. I had a pressing desire to pray and read His Word.

There was also an emotional churning within me that would not stop. I found great comfort through reading the Psalms and studying how David gave himself completely to the Lord. He held nothing back, and this is exactly what God wanted me to do—give all of myself to Him. Over a few weeks He revealed to me that He was indeed going to move me. Even though I did not like the idea, I surrendered myself to Him. And the moment I said yes, the inner churning in my spirit stopped. The way I discovered God's will for my life was through submitting and studying what the Bible had to say about situations similar to my own. The way I learned to obey was through prayer, surrender to God, and also by continuing to read about the lives of men and women who gave themselves to be used by God.

God's Spirit gives us discernment. What we believe about God determines how we live! Far too many believers go through life without being grounded in the Word of God. They take a wrong turn because they have not taken time to learn what God wants them to do. I could have said no to the Lord and not moved to Atlanta, but think of the blessing I would have missed. At the time of my decision, I had never visited the city. I had driven through on my way to another destination, but I did not know anything about it. One day while I was praying, it was as if I saw the skyline of the city within my mind.

A dark cloud was positioned over it. My heart sank because I knew God was forewarning me that while this was His will, I was going to have a hard time in my new ministry. This has been true, but I would not change a thing concerning my ministry in Atlanta. God has done amazing things, but if I had refused to obey Him, I never would have experienced His blessings in so many ways. Nor would I have learned all that I have over these thirty-plus years. I took time to ask God to show me His will through His Word. The discernment I needed for this situation and all the others in my life came as a result of studying the Word of God. We can have "common" sense, but it is so much more advantageous to have godly discernment. When difficulty comes, we can turn back the pages of time in our minds and remind the Lord that He brought us this far and we believe that He will carry us on from here.

The apostle Paul writes, "Rejoice always; pray without ceasing; in everything give thanks; for this is God's will for you in Christ Jesus. Do not quench the Spirit; do not despise prophetic utterances. But examine everything carefully; hold fast to that which is good; abstain from every form of evil" (1 Thess. 5:16–22). One of the ways you quench God's Spirit is when you ignore His call. He may be leading you to spend time in the morning with Him in prayer and Bible study. For days and weeks, you have felt a sense of drawing within your heart and you keep saying, "I'll do it tomorrow." If you do not have a godly grid system within your thought processes, then you cannot detect error and will be drawn away into all kinds of erroneous thinking and ventures. The Word of God was given to us, not only to lead us into salvation, but also to lead us into a godly way of life. If we are to have lives that reflect God's love and grace to others, we must know Him and His truth.

Years ago I met an older woman who began to tell me how long she had been a Christian. She talked about the size of the church she attended and the degrees her pastor had. "We can seat over fifteen hundred in our sanctuary," she said proudly. Suddenly I was struck with one thought: *I don't want to know about a church building. I want to know about Christ's life within you. What is He teaching you? Are you learning more about Him each day? Have you developed an awesome relationship with Him that goes beyond anything we can have this side of heaven?* Buildings are places where we gather to worship the Lord, but God's temple is within the lives of those who love Him.

Are you living to know Him? If you are, then you will have ✓ a single desire welling up within you and that will be to "come" to Him. Like Moses, you will say, "I must turn aside now and see this marvelous sight."

CHAPTER 2

LIVE A SURRENDERED LIFE

The burning bush encounter was a critical juncture in Moses' life. Not only was it the place where he was drawn to the Lord; it also was a place of ultimate surrender to God. When we read through Exodus 3, one of the things we notice is how God addressed every issue Moses had considered while in Egypt and probably during the years he was in the wilderness. It was as if God worked His way down Moses' list and then said, "Here is what I am going to do and what I want you to do." There was no time to argue. The Lord was ready to go to work. Moses was being given marching orders, and he could either say yes or no, but he wasn't given an opportunity to debate God's will with Him. He did ask God to tell him who was sending him. I believe Moses knew better than to refuse God's call.

He approached the burning bush and immediately the Lord instructed him to remove his sandals. From the start, God wanted Moses to know He was holy and worthy of honor and respect. People ask me, "How can I learn to study the Bible effectively?" The best way to begin is with unconditional surrender—on your face before the Lord in prayer. The Word of God is very clear to those who come to Him with open, submissive hearts. However, if we are consumed by the pressures of life and come to Him demanding that He answer a list of questions that we deem as being important, we will never experience what Moses did standing in God's awesome presence. He is not "on call" for us. Instead, He calls us to come to Him with an open heart.

UNCONDITIONAL SURRENDER

Moses realized he was in the presence of holiness. He did not stop and think about how it would feel to have sand in his shoes, nor did he consider whether or not he would step on something that could hurt his feet. The most important thing to him at that moment was bowing down before the God of the universe. Our decision to trust Christ as our personal Savior was a starting point. God's goal is for us to live unconditionally surrendered to Him every day of our lives. If you study the life of Moses, you will find that many times, he had as much difficulty doing this as we do. But he never turned away from God. He experienced times of frustration that even led to sin. Yet he always honored God by seeking His restoration and forgiveness.

Surrender to Christ is a necessary part of the Christian life. Moses surrendered to hear God's voice. This is what He calls us to do as we read and study His Word each day. Moses obeyed the Lord because he realized very quickly that he was being led to do something he longed to accomplish. Often we hear people talk about not wanting to submit to God's will because they are afraid of what He might require of them. This is very sad because people run the risk of missing God's best for their lives. Usually, when God leads us to do something, He places a desire for it within our hearts. Then if we are sensitive to His Spirit, we will hear His voice leading and motivating us to walk in a certain direction. Regardless of where this leads, obeying God is better than any sacrifice you could offer Him later in life. Reading and studying Scripture provides the perfect atmosphere for God to reveal Himself and His promises to us. Worry, doubt, and fear fade as we say yes to Him. How do you surrender your life and your concerns to God?

Realize your need. Moses had heard of the Lord, but it wasn't until he stood in front of the burning bush that he realized his need for God. He could not do what the Lord was asking him to do on his own. Neither can we. Life's challenges require God's intervention and power. The Lord spoke to Abraham, and he obeyed. God called to Moses, and he submitted his life to the Lord. Joseph knew the Lord had something special in mind for his life, but he had to learn to trust God even when it appeared that there was no hope for his future. David was the anointed king over Israel, yet he also waited for years to see this become a reality. But he waited, he obeyed, and he did not say no. Jesus called His disciples, and none refused the call. None of the twelve said, "Let me think about it overnight and I'll get back with you." When God calls, we need to respond.

✓ *Recognize God's call.* God desires our fellowship. He doesn't need our fellowship in order to be God, but He desires it. Surrender does not mean we stop living. In fact, if you go through God's Word and study the lives of the people who followed Him, you quickly realize each one lived a highly productive life. The apostle Paul was a Jewish scholar who studied under Gamaliel— one of the most highly respected rabbis of his day. Yet nothing Paul learned in this man's classroom compared to what he learned in the presence of God. You have the same awesome opportunity to study God's truth. If there is a need for wisdom, He provides it. Yet I watch people live lives that are partially surrendered and never quite achieve the goals the Lord has for them.

✓ Unconditional surrender means there are no restrictions. Nothing is held back—there is total yielding of everything to the control of Jesus Christ. Churches are filled with members who are saved but not surrendered, and they wonder why they cannot hear God's voice or why He is not using them to a greater degree. They don't understand why the Christian life seems like a struggle. When they try to serve the Lord, the power of the Holy Spirit is not upon them because their lives are not fully committed. They are conditionally surrendered.

Recall His goodness. In times of surrender, one of the best things you can do is to take refuge in the Word of God. The psalmist writes, "Cast your burden upon the LORD and He will sustain you; He will never allow the righteous to be shaken" (Ps. 55:22). And Psalm 56:3–4 says, "When I am afraid, I will put my trust in You. In God, whose word I praise, in God I have put my trust; I shall not be afraid. What can mere man do to me?" There are thousands of promises in God's Word, but if you never open His Word, you are defenseless when the enemy attacks. You may think, *God is good. Surely He will protect me.* This way of reasoning has so much more power when you can say, "The LORD is my shepherd, I shall not want. He makes me lie down in green pastures; He leads me beside quiet waters. He restores my soul" (Ps. 23:1–3).

There is infinite power and hope in God's Word. His goodness to us comes alive whenever we read the Scriptures. Without their truth, we have no direction for our lives. We float along like a rudderless ship tossed one way and then another by the storms of life. The prophet Jeremiah gives insight into the way God wants us to live: "Call to Me and I will answer you, and I will tell you great and mighty things, which you do not know" (33:3). If you want to learn how to study God's Word, the first thing you must do is to come to the Lord, and the second is to surrender your life to Him.

One of the reasons we fail to do this is due to feelings of fear—

✓ we are afraid to give up control. We become fearful over the thought of someone else calling all the plays for our lives. But who is better qualified to do this than God? No one is. I understand how feelings can come into play in our lives, but we must remain focused on the truth of God. Circumstances are not always pleasant, and some can be frightening when they first occur, but we must not allow Satan to plant seeds of doubt in our hearts. If we do, he will continue to water them with negative, hopeless thoughts in an effort to narrow our worlds to a point where we are no longer living a life of faith. Instead, we are walking by the light of our own fires, and the result is torment of heart and mind (Isa. 50:11).

WHY SURRENDER MY LIFE?

The young man looked at me as if I were speaking a foreign language. He was determined to marry a young woman who did not love him. His insecurities had driven him to the point of thinking that "this was it." Either he married now or he never would. He did not want to take time to seek God's guidance. So he came to me hoping that I would give him the answer that he desperately wanted. It did not happen, because I pointed him to God, encouraging him to pray and study His Word. No matter what our need is, God has an answer. No situation is too complicated for Him to handle. Nothing is beyond His ability to communicate His truth to our hearts. But, we must be open to hear what He has to say.

What does living a life of surrender mean? It means that we refuse to allow fear or any other <u>negative emotion</u> to control us. We make a choice to trust God for the needs we have, including the future and all it contains. We also refuse to yield to the criticism of others. What does criticism have to do with studying God's Word? Everything! If Satan cannot get you off course one way, he will double back and try something different, and many times hearing what others are saying about us does the trick. However, if we are going to serve God, then we must come to a point where we want His approval over that of the world.

Ask God to expose the pride and rebellion in your heart. Both of these will prevent us from having a true hunger for God's Word. Instead of focusing on Christ and asking Him to shape our lives so we are honoring to Him, we may spend time thinking about how others are acting or what they are not doing. Often, while counseling individuals, I have to stop people who are complaining about the way they have been treated by a spouse, coworker, boss, or friend and have a reality check with them. It is as if they have forgotten the grace God has extended to them. When I suggest that they recall God's goodness to them, there is always hesitation because it is clear where our conversation is going.

The study of God's grace within His Word helps us gain a right perspective of our lives while eradicating pride from our hearts. If you have a hard time forgiving another person, more than likely you will have a hard time accepting God's love and forgiveness for your own life. You must experience His forgiveness in order to be able to forgive others. Often, people say they have forgiven those who have hurt them but fail to do so. The hurt is deep, and they try to hold the other person hostage and account-able for the hurt he or she has inflicted. Those who forgive and allow God to heal their wounds are the ones who gain a great victory. Instead of stewing in anger, they go on with life and can read and study God's Word without battling thoughts of getting even. Don't be deceived: pride thrives in an atmosphere of unforgiveness. It resists surrender and will stop at nothing to prevent a believer from yielding his or her life fully to Jesus Christ, because Satan knows that a surrendered life is one that God uses to do great things.

I'm not going to tell you that living a life of surrender is easy. However, I will tell you there is nothing that compares to the joy that comes as a result of living a life abandoned to Jesus Christ. Surrender has the ability to heal broken relationships, open the door to forgiveness, and teach us more about God than any other action we could take. It is an essential step in studying God's Word.

Jesus surrendered His life for you and me. He is our living sacrifice—the very person who has overcome sin and death. When you feel God is leading you to surrender an emotion or a feeling or an activity, remember that you don't have to be in con-trol, because God is totally and masterfully in control of your life. You can live free in Him because He is over all things. On more than one occasion, people have told me, "I can't let go!" Panic filled their eyes, and I told them that until they did, they would continue to be in a tug-of-war with God for ultimate control. And the truth is: He never loses. We lose because we waste precious time worrying and holding on to something that we can never have—control.

The results of surrender are:

- Maximum blessing
- Maximum usefulness
- Maximum fellowship with God
- Maximum power due to the unrestricted flow of the Spirit of God within our lives as believers

In some cases, surrender becomes a moment-by-moment activity. Live long enough and you will find that there are times when you know God is telling you to give Him this area of your life or this attitude, but you deliberately and willfully ignore Him and try to go on as if nothing is wrong. You get up in the morning, read your devotional, pray, and leave for work or begin your day at home with the children. Before long, however, you sense a "dryness" forming in your spirit. You wonder where God is. Has He abandoned you? Is He angry? The answer is no. He is waiting for you to make the right decision and do what He has instructed you to do. There are people who have ignored God for years, and they have suffered emotionally, physically, and spiritually as a result of their decision. A lack of surrender is a flag of defeat announcing our unbelief in God's ability to rescue and keep us safe. But we do not have to live like this. The friends I talk with who are Christian psychologists tell me that we benefit greatly from just letting go and allowing God to be God in our lives.

How do you make a full surrender so that you can live and study God's Word to the maximum?

✓ *Recognize that God has the right to require us to lay down our lives before Him.*

✓ *Make a deliberate, willful decision to relinquish control of your life*—every area and all that concerns you.

Be willing to receive what He wants to give you. The enemy will tell you that if you surrender, you will lose everything. Remember that when he speaks, he speaks his native language. In other words, he lies (John 8:44). The truth is that when you ✓ surrender to Christ, you step across the threshold of infinite blessing. You may or may not see this immediately, but the blessings will come. Moses led the people out of Egypt, David ascended to the throne, Joseph was released from prison, Daniel was lifted out of the lions' den, Paul made it to Rome, Peter was released from prison, and Jesus arose from the grave. Nothing is impossible with God—absolutely nothing. But it all

begins with surrender and a desire to know God. Is this your
prayer: "God, teach me more about Yourself"? If it is, then surrender will come naturally. You may have times of resistance,
but God is patient and He will send the right amount of pressure to position you for surrender and blessing.

CHAPTER 3

STUDY TO BE YOUR BEST

We live in an age when we can enter a couple of keystrokes on our computers and within seconds the world is available online in front of us. We can turn on a television and watch a news report as it unfolds on the other side of the globe. In fact, we can do almost anything from a technological sense and never leave home. Information comes and goes so quickly that it is overwhelming at times. Yet when you think about it, people are becoming more disenchanted with life every day. They have the world at their fingertips, but they are not happy. Their lives are restless, void of joy and peace. They search for something— anything to create an atmosphere of contentment within their hearts—but all their efforts end in frustration. It is not enough to own the largest home, the fastest car, the best laptop, or the newest media player. People want more—more gadgets, more things to keep them busy in an effort to fill the gaps in their lives.

The Gods of This Age

From the world's perspective, significance may be a goal to gain, but from God's point of view, it is vanity and "striving after wind" (Eccl. 4:4). The more we strive to gain attention, power, prominence, and wealth, the more distractions gather in and around our lives and the greater the potential for us to drift in our faith. There are people who have great wealth and love the Lord deeply. They have learned an important lesson: God first and above all things.

The gods of this age include anything that creates a distance between God and us. As silly as it may sound, we can be guilty of worshiping something as simple as an electronic game or the latest telephone device. After all, what is an idol? It is something we worship in place of the Lord. It includes the pursuit of money, power, beauty, or a relationship that is not God's best for us. Certainly, other people can become idols to us if our lives are caught up in them and not in the Lord. An idol is something that we must have and something that causes us to redirect our thinking away from the One who is the only source of our worship. We can choose to spend time with things that are not His best, or we can choose to walk in His presence. When we make a wrong choice, we open our lives up to something that can prevent us from developing a personal relationship with the Savior. It grabs our attention and affection—two things that God desires of us. He also wants our love, devotion, and friendship.

Satan's primary goal is to prevent us from having an intimate relationship with the Lord. He wants to derail our love and devotion for God. One of the ways he does this is by filling our time with distractions and the very things that prevent us from studying God's Word. Why does he go to such lengths? Because he knows that if we study God's Word, we will discover the joy, peace, security, and blessing of being with God. He knows that God will strengthen us as we read His Word and prepare us for life's difficult challenges. In essence, we will learn how to "bend a bow of bronze" (Ps. 18:34). We will learn how to discern the truth about the enemy, who is a liar, a deceiver, and the prince of darkness. His folly will be exposed as God's Spirit teaches us how to stand firm in our faith. With God's Word as our sword and shield, we will take captive every thought that would exalt itself above Jesus Christ.

THE TRANSFORMING TRUTH OF GOD'S WORD

The prophet Isaiah writes, "For as the heavens are higher than the earth, so are My ways higher than your ways and My thoughts than your thoughts" (55:9). There is no book to match God's Word because it contains the mind of God. He gave it to us so we could know and understand:

- His ways
- His character
- His attitude

- His power
- His love
- His forgiveness
- His eternal gift of salvation
- His hope

God's Word has the ability to teach us how to know Him intimately, how to communicate with Him, how to be forgiven of sin, how to live successfully, and how to die unafraid because Jesus has faced death and overcome it. Yet how many times have we stopped at a traffic light and noticed a Bible carelessly tossed in the back window of the car in front of us? Or how many times have we visited a friend's house only to find that there is no Bible in sight?

If I gave you fifty thousand dollars in a shoebox and told you that you could do whatever you wanted to do with the money, would you just shove it on the shelf and forget about it? No! More than likely, some would invest it and others would immediately spend every dollar. It would be used. The living Word of God is more valuable than anything this world can offer us. There is more within its pages than any amount of money can buy. I'm convinced that the reason people do not read the Bible more is because Satan has blinded them to the truth. He tells them they don't need to be concerned about what God has to say. They can think for themselves. They don't need advice from Him. Or there are situations where believers simply don't take the time to seek godly wisdom. They are ignorant and do not realize the vast amount of truth and hope they have at their fingertips

You can purchase the latest edition of the Bible, but if you rarely open it, you will never know the truth it contains. The way we handle His Word reflects the value we place on it. If we value its message, then we will want to study it and use it every day. When our hearts are turned toward Him in prayer, His words— the words we read within the text of the Bible—bring fresh insight to our problems, fears, and dreams. His truth comforts us in times of trouble, brings encouragement when we are tempted to doubt, and provides the guidance we need to make godly, wise decisions.

I also have heard people say, "I have had my Bible for years, and it is still like brand new." If you are not reading your Bible every day, then you are not living a godly life. You want the Bible you have to be well-worn and filled with notations chronicling what God has done in your life, as well as the promises He has given you for the future. When a person begins to understand the benefit of the Bible, he or she won't allow it to be pristine for very long. I'm not talking about misusing it; I'm talking about using it to the fullest. The dirtier its pages become, the more evident it is that you are reading with a desire to find an answer to your needs as well as get to know Him and His ways. Most people protect and never use the things that have great value to them, but in this case, the very thing that has the greatest value should be used to the maximum every day.

THE BENEFITS OF STUDYING GOD'S WORD

Peter writes, "You have been born again not of seed which is perishable but imperishable, that is, through the living and enduring word of God" (1 Pet. 1:23). God's Word is eternal. You can watch and listen to as much of today's news as you want and not receive truth. God is the ultimate newsmaker—not a politician, a president, a prime minister, a king, or a queen. God is over all things. Now, we need to live and be wise in our decisions. We cannot check out on our social responsibilities, but we also need to know that there is a much larger plan in place other than what we see reported. No one is going to report the fact that God is at work, and He knows exactly how to handle any financial and political turmoil in years to come.

There are many benefits to studying God's Word.

Scripture teaches us how to develop a close, personal relationship with the Savior. As we study His Word and apply it to our lives, we let go of many of the sins that have the potential to harm our fellowship with Him. We begin to establish a "right" relationship with the Savior—one that is based on His eternal love, forgiveness, and grace. It is a relationship that leads to our salvation and sets us free from the bondage of sin.

The Bible is our guide. The psalmist writes, "Your word is a lamp to my feet and a light to my path" (119:105). When you want to find direction for your life, one of the simplest things you can do is to pick up God's Word and ask the Lord to give you His guidance for your circumstances. Don't just open it up and read the first thing that you see on a page. This is not true Bible study. Studying God's Word means taking a planned break from the rushed and often frantic pace of your life and asking God to speak to your heart so that you will hear what He wants you to do.

He turns our grief into peace and joy through reading His Word. When you and I are struggling and we open God's Word, we discover some amazing truths: He loves us no matter what we have done in the past. He cares about us and has a plan for our futures, and He has promised to walk through every difficulty beside us. In other words, He will not abandon us. I don't know about you, but when I think about the omnipotent God of the universe loving me with an intimate love, my heart is instantly refreshed and infused with immeasurable hope and joy.

The Word of God is our peace. From a dark and lonely jail cell the apostle Paul writes, "Be anxious for nothing, but in everything by prayer and supplication with thanksgiving let your requests be made known to God. And the peace of God, which surpasses all comprehension, will guard your hearts and your minds in Christ Jesus" (Phil. 4:6–7). When you have a relationship with Jesus Christ, no matter what you are going through, you will have a deep, abiding sense of joy. This does not mean you will not feel the stress or pressure of the moment. However, when you are by yourself, you will know that you are not alone and that God is with you, sustaining you, and this will be an anchor of peace to your heart. He will never withhold His good-ness from you. When we are going through hardship and we need a sense of divine peace, God calms our souls and hearts through the reading of His Word. He gives us a peace that pass-es all human understanding.

God's Word convicts us of sin. The author of Hebrews writes, "For the word of God is living and active and sharper than any two-edged sword, and piercing as far as the division of soul and spirit, of both joints and marrow, and able to judge the thoughts and intentions of the heart" (4:12). At times people try desper-ately to hide their motives from others. Deep inside they are fighting an ominous battle with feelings of pride, jealousy, and envy. On the outside they appear cool and unruffled by life, but under the surface their emotions are a ticking time bomb wait-ing to explode. Friends and family may not know of their strug-gle, but God does.

If our foremost desire is to please God, then we will confess the things that He points out and ask Him to teach us how to live life in step with the principles in His Word. He knows we cannot achieve this quickly. Therefore, He begins to teach us just enough for us to notice the change in our hearts and to desire a deeper relationship with Him. There will be times of failure when we feel as though we are living life in reverse, but actually the more submitted our lives become, the more we are advancing in our spiritual walk with Him.

The Word of God protects us from evil. "How can a young man keep his way pure? By keeping it according to Your word" (Ps. 119:9). This one line written by the psalmist pretty much sums up how we need to live our lives—in God's purity and according to the precepts of His Word. Then we read the psalmist's heartfelt prayer, "With all my heart I have sought You; do not let me wander from Your commandments. Your word I have treasured in my heart, that I may not sin against You" (vv. 10–11). When you hide God's Word in your heart, He uses it to build up a resistance to sin. He gives us insight into potentially problematic situations and provides godly discernment about how to handle them. God's Word shines a convicting light on our sinfulness. His goal is not to frighten us but to prevent us from drifting in our thoughts and faith, because He knows that when this happens we become easy targets for discouragement. But when you program your life according to the Word of God, you will recognize potential problems even before they unfold.

The Bible offers us eternal hope. When you feel hopeless, the best thing you can do is not to think about the future. That may seem odd to you, but many people drift into a cycle of hopelessness because they do not feel they will accomplish the goals they wanted for their lives. First, they have forgotten that nothing is too difficult for the Lord (Jer. 32:17). All things are possible for Him (Luke 1:37). They have bypassed any lesson of faith that they have learned earlier because faith in God tells us that we will not be disappointed (Ps. 22:5).

You have no idea what tomorrow will hold, but one thing is sure: it will be wonderful because God is involved. You may think, *You don't know my situation.* The truth is, I don't. But likewise, you do not know the heartache I have had to deal with and the times I have wondered if I would be able to continue. Each time I felt hopeless, I got on my face before the Lord with an ✓ open Bible and prayed, "God, You know my circumstances, and I know You also know what I'm feeling. Please encourage me and show me the way through this narrow place in my life." Without fail, God always directs my steps. I may have to be willing to change my course or wait on His timing, but He always answers my prayers. When you have a personal relationship with the God of the universe, you have it all—nothing is more dynamic than this! And nothing and no one has the ability to guard your heart the way He does because He is your shield and eternal defender.

God's Word instructs us. It is impossible to grow in your Christian life apart from reading the Bible. We need to be fed a steady diet from His Word. I'm a big supporter of taking vitamins and minerals. I walk a couple of miles every day, if not farther. I believe in staying in shape, eating well, and taking care of the body God has given me. However, one day, no matter what any of us do, our bodies will die, but our spirits will live for eternity. It is amazing to me how many people put so much emphasis on the way they look and the amount of exercise they do each day, but they never open God's Word. They are physically healthy, but spiritually they are weak and even sick. Some people live a lifetime never enjoying the awesome workout of being in God's Word and watching it come to life within them.

God's Word should be read every day. Effectiveness is what most Christians want—they want to be effective in their walk with Christ and in their knowledge of God. However, they fail to do one important thing and that is to read the instruction manual. Some people tell me they like to read through the Bible every year. This is one way to become familiar with God's Word.

When I talk about reading Scripture, I'm talking about studying Scripture and asking God to open your mind and heart to His truth. To do this, you don't necessarily need to follow a set pattern, but you do need to follow God's Spirit. You can begin where your greatest need is. You may need a word of encouragement. Studying King David's life along with the many psalms he wrote would certainly help you gain insight into this subject. If you are feeling like an outcast, then read 2 Samuel and a few of the psalms David wrote while hiding from King Saul. Suddenly you will feel encouraged because you will realize that if God delivered David, He will deliver you—and He will. This is just an example of how to begin. Once you open the pages of His priceless book, He becomes committed to revealing not only Himself to you but also His deepest truth.

God's Word teaches us to meditate on its truth. After you have started reading Scripture on a regular basis, the Holy Spirit will begin to bring to mind a special verse that seems to turn up over and over again. When you think of this passage, write it down on a three-by-five-inch card and take it with you. Commit the verse to memory and allow your mind to meditate on it during the day. Do this for three weeks, and I promise that your life will be changed. I can't explain why three weeks is important; I just know it works. Meditation is the most important thing we can do when studying God's Word. Through this we learn how to focus on His truth anywhere and any place.

Reading God's Word leads to study and tremendous insight. Get a concordance or a set of commentaries and study the passages of Scripture that God brings to mind or that you hear at church. Ask the Lord to reveal His truth to you concerning what you are reading. One way the Bible can come to life is when you begin to dig deeper into the background of a verse. Scholars study each word, and there are tools available to help you do the same thing. In writing to Timothy, Paul tells him, "Be diligent to present yourself approved to God as a workman who does not need to be ashamed, accurately handling the word of truth" (2 Tim. 2:15).

Nothing excites me more than when God brings some word to mind and I start to trail after it in Scripture. I move from the Old Testament to the New Testament looking up how many times it appears in Scripture and what it means in light of the text that I am studying. If you commit yourself to the study of God's Word, an entirely new adventure will open up before you.

The study of Scripture teaches us to believe and trust God. The Bible is infallible. It is true and never contradicts itself. If you believe what He has given you in Scripture, you will not only live a blessed life, you will be informed and have tremendous wisdom and discernment.

The Word of God teaches us how to apply His truth to our lives. When you buy a new car, you never leave it sitting in your driveway; you take it out on the road. And this is what you should do when it comes to the truth and the principles in God's Word. Some people are spiritual pygmies. They accept Christ as their Savior and that is it. They never grow spiritually. Every little wind of adversity blows them first one way and then another because they have not hidden God's Word in their hearts. You will never know the ways of God until you get a glimpse of what He is really like. You will never know the peace that comes as a result of trusting Him and knowing that He holds your life in His righteous right hand.

CHAPTER 4

LISTEN FOR GOD'S VOICE

I remember when I was a teenager my mother would tell me, "We're going to serve supper at six o'clock. So be here then." I would say, "Yes, ma'am," but later I would become so involved in playing with my friends that I would forget to check what time it was. Then I would hear her calling, "Charles, Charles." I could be half a block away from my house and it would not matter; I knew her voice. In fact, I'm convinced that several moms could have called out my name and I still would have been able to distinguish hers. Why? I knew her voice. I grew up listening to her. When she called my name, I answered. I didn't ignore her because I loved her and I knew that she would not call to me unless she really needed me to come. Can you say the same thing when it comes to answering God's call? Jesus said, "My sheep hear My voice, and I know them, and they follow Me" (John 10:27). God wants us to learn how to discern His voice so we will be able to understand His Word and apply its principles to our lives.

√ When we become sensitive to God's voice, He can speak to us through His Word, and suddenly we are aware of His will for our lives or circumstances. Recognizing His voice is not difficult, but you must have a desire to hear Him and learn how to be still within your heart so you can follow where He leads. There are times when the Lord gives us direction and guidance about a situation, and it is critical for us to listen so we will make the correct decisions. We want to be certain that what we hear is from Him and not from the enemy or a result of something we have conceived in our own minds. When it comes to making wise decisions, there are many variables. This is why it is crucial to pray and read God's Word.

Do You Know the Sound of God's Voice?

You may be on the verge of making a huge decision and think you know what you should do. However, you wonder, *What if something goes wrong? What if God has another plan? What happens if I make a mistake? Will God forgive me?* I am asked questions like these often, especially when a potential decision about marriage is involved. God's will is not a mystery. It is something He wants us to know, just as He wants us to understand the principles in His Word. We must make a choice to learn His ways, and this means learning to hear His voice.

√ We get into trouble when we allow our minds to drift away from the things of God and become concerned about the things of this world. <u>God wants us to learn how to hear His voice so that we</u> can make wise, godly decisions instead of making choices based on what the world tells us is right and acceptable. <u>How do we do this?</u> There are several steps, but before we can look at these, we need to underscore the fact that God's ways are not man's ways. "'For My thoughts are not your thoughts, nor are your ways My ways,' declares the LORD. 'For as the heavens are higher than the earth, so are My ways higher than your ways and My thoughts than your thoughts'" (Isa. 55:8–9). Sometimes we are caught in a bad situation. We find ourselves in the middle of a crisis and wonder, *Lord, how can You use this for Your glory? Everything seems so dark and hopeless.* But God knows the way through the storm. He has a plan that often is hidden from view. When this is the case, He calls us to walk by faith—trusting Him to lead us through the difficulty safely or to make the right decision.

One student explained to me how he had trusted God to show him the college he should attend. "When I was in high school, I did not think about going to college. My grades were not the best and I just put it off. Then a couple of years after I graduated, I sensed the Lord calling me into full-time ministry. At first I thought I had made a mistake, but after asking Him to confirm His call in His Word, I changed my mind. He repeatedly made it clear that He wanted me to enter the ministry." When God calls a person to a certain task, He also prepares him or her for the work. <u>Submitting to God's call is the first step.</u> The second includes time spent in prayer and reading God's Word. He will lead us each step of the way, but we must seek Him, listen for His instruction, and then obey Him.

LEARNING TO HEAR GOD'S VOICE

1. There have been times in my life when something happened and immediately a verse of Scripture came to mind. This is how God
2. speaks to us. Or perhaps I have been thinking about a decision and praying for wisdom when I heard God's still, small voice reminding me of a truth that I learned in His Word. There are several ways you can discern whether or not the voice you are hearing is from God.

1. *God's voice is always consistent with Scripture.* He never contradicts His Word. I remember when my children, Andy and Becky, were young, they would try to talk me into allowing them to do things that I really did not feel were God's best. Usually only one of them would show up at the door of my study asking to talk with me. On one occasion they came together with a request that I knew was not what I wanted them to do. I listened and then told them, "Let's pray about it, and we'll see what God has to say." We prayed, and then I asked them to continue praying for a few days and we would discuss it again. Three days later they were back with a word from God. They believed it was His will for them to go forward with this certain decision. I knew in my spirit that it was not what God wanted. So I had to explain

why their decision was not right. What they wanted to do contradicted God's Word. Often we can want something so badly that we convince ourselves it is what God wants for us too. This is why it is extremely important for us to be willing to relinquish our desires to God and what He has revealed in His Word. This may be the most difficult thing you will do, but it is necessary and something He requires of you and me. Later Andy and Becky admitted that deep inside they had also felt "checked" in their spirits by God. The thought of missing an opportunity motivated them to believe that God would be okay with it— even if their decision was a wrong one.

Many times, God's truth will conflict with human reasoning. 2.
The death of Christ did not make sense from a human standpoint. But from God's perspective, it did. We do not know all that He knows. He is infinite in wisdom, and our knowledge is limited and finite. We may think we know a great deal, but we do not know what will happen tomorrow, or the next day, or the following month. However, God does. He knows this, and He knows how to set the pattern for our lives so we stay perfectly in line with His will and receive His greatest blessings.

a. He will never lead us into sin.

b. He will not ask us to do anything that results in disobedience.

c. He will never tempt or confuse us. These are Satan's acts of sinful folly.

In Matthew 16, we see the stark contrast between godly

knowledge and earthly reasoning. In the first half of this chapter, Peter confesses that Jesus is "the Christ, the Son of the living God" (v. 16). And Jesus commends His disciple's sensitivity to God: "Blessed are you, Simon Barjona, because flesh and blood did not reveal this to you, but My Father who is in heaven" (v. 17). Less than three verses later, we read how Peter did a complete turnaround—he ignored what the Spirit of God had told him and basically cried out, "What? How can You, being the Messiah, submit to being killed by the elders, chief priests, and scribes? There is no way that fits! Everything I have been taught makes it clear the Messiah will come and save His people from oppression. We are oppressed; I'm oppressed. Don't talk about dying and leaving us. Not now, not after we have come so far and done so much!"

Instead of becoming worried over what could happen, we can open His Word and read, "Trust in the LORD with all your heart and do not lean on your own understanding. In all your ways acknowledge Him, and He will make your paths straight" (Prov. 3:5–6). God wants us to live by faith and not feelings. This does not mean we stop thinking or working through problems. But it does mean that when we cannot figure something out, we continue to go the way that we believe God is calling us to travel without questioning His guidance.

God's voice will never stir up our fleshly nature. When you and I walk in obedience to Christ, life becomes more exciting the older we become and the longer we walk with Him. There is nothing dull about the Christian life. Yet many believers mistakenly believe that to enjoy life, they need to live like the world lives. They need to go to R-rated movies, drink, flirt, and ignore God's principles except on Sunday. Monday through Saturday they live the way they choose, but on Sunday, life changes. During the week they ignore God's Word and His truth and yield to Satan's suggestion that life lived as a believer in Jesus Christ is boring. Nothing could be further from the truth. There is nothing dull about living free of sin and shame.

God's voice will challenge us to trust Him in a greater way. Peter and the disciples had a choice: either they could trust God and believe in His eternal promises, or they could push for human results. This is what Judas did—he tried to pressure Jesus into revealing Himself as an earthly Messiah. His intentions were worse than Peter's, and he ended up handing Jesus over to the authorities to be crucified. There will be situations when life changes quickly. The disciples could not believe what they were hearing when Jesus told them that He was going to die. Maybe you have received some bad news and you are wondering what you will do. You thought you had everything figured out for the future, but now the outlook is gray and cloudy. Or is it? The disciples thought their ministry was over, but it had just begun. They were sure the crucifixion was a dead end, but in reality it was a new beginning. Their faith was challenged and turned out to be small. However, as they regained their hope through time spent with the risen Lord, it was perfected. Taking time to study God's Word resets our minds and hearts on eternal things. Then when problems come, we know to pick up His Word and ask Him to show us how to respond correctly. Peter learned to respond and not react. He also learned how to trust God and live by faith, even if his circumstances did not make sense.

Studying God's Word and applying His principles to our lives takes courage. Joshua knew what he needed to do. Moses had given him strict instructions, but he allowed fear to creep into his life. He did not have God's Word like we have it today. This may have been one of the reasons that the Lord appeared to him before he led the nation of Israel into battle at Jericho. God told him, "Have I not commanded you? Be strong and courageous! Do not tremble or be dismayed, for the LORD your God is with you wherever you go" (Josh. 1:9). Joshua was Moses' understudy. He was with him for years and witnessed God's work through Moses. When Moses died, the Lord chose Joshua to take his place.

Accepting this call took great courage on Joshua's part. But he had been with Moses and witnessed what the Lord did for the nation of Israel. He was present when God parted the Red Sea. He had been awestruck by God's mighty power. Yet even Joshua needed to be reminded of the source of his faith: "Remember the word which Moses the servant of the LORD commanded you, saying, 'The LORD your God gives you rest and will give you this land'" (Josh. 1:13). God was saying to His servant, "Remember the words you have been given—the godly counsel you have gained at the feet of Moses, My servant, and don't give up. I will fulfill the promises I have given you; be courageous!"

God's voice may require us to be patient and still. Most of us like easy solutions, quick answers, and fast service. Few people actually enjoy waiting. Yet this is what David learned to do in God's presence. He waited before the Lord so that he would know His will. He didn't just jump ahead without knowing what God wanted him to do. David writes, "I waited patiently for the LORD; and He inclined to me and heard my cry. He brought me up out of the pit of destruction, out of the miry clay, and He set my feet upon a rock making my footsteps firm. He put a new song in my mouth, a song of praise to our God; many will see and fear and will trust in the LORD" (Ps. 40:1–3).

It is fun to get an instant answer to a need, but there is an even greater reward in learning how to wait patiently in faith for God's answer to your prayer. David waited years before he saw God's promise to him become a reality. It was forty years before the nation of Israel entered the Promised Land, Joseph was in prison for years, and even Daniel's night in the lions' den seemed far too lengthy; but God sustained those who trusted Him—those who believed in His faithfulness. There is only one way to learn about God's goodness, grace, and mercy toward you, and that is through reading His Word—not quickly or at a glance—

and taking time to study and to ask Him to show you what He wants you to learn and apply to your life.

The study of God's Word brings eternal benefits. Your life begins to change immediately the moment you seriously begin reading and memorizing Scripture. You are putting the eternal Word of God into your life. You gain access to His throne room and begin to understand the way He thinks. I have met believers who have never taken time to study God's Word. They go to church and never write down a single thing they hear. They rarely read God's Word and only quote Scriptures that fit their personal desires. They are milk-fed Christians, but God wants us to discover the real food He has to offer (1 Cor. 3:2).

God's voice provides wisdom. Jesus told His followers, "I do nothing on My own initiative, but I speak these things as the Father taught Me" (John 8:28). Even the Son of God, the living Word of God, learned from the words given to Him by God. And He did not speak from His own point of view but from the Father's. The Bible is infallible because it is God's Word. This is not debatable. All Scripture is inspired by God for His purposes. He placed His words in the minds and hearts of the men who recorded them. There is nothing that has ever been written to compare with the Word of God—no other book has lasted as long and proven to be true the way the Bible has. Whatever your circumstances, God has a word of encouragement for you waiting in His Word. You could be celebrating a great joy. If so, God celebrates with you: "The LORD your God is with you, he is mighty to save. He will take great delight in you, he will quiet you with his love, he will rejoice over you with singing" (Zeph. 3:17 NIV).

God uses Scripture. Many times when I have been praying about something, suddenly within my spirit I have heard a soft voice. It could be one or two words, but it is enough to cause me to think of a Scripture that fits my situation. One time I needed an answer from God about a decision that I needed to make. I had prayed and read His Word and also taken notes on what I had studied. I always keep a pad and pencil beside my Bible to write down what God is showing me through His Word. I may sense my interest being drawn to a certain section, and before I know it, I have moved from Scripture to Scripture studying and recording one principle or truth after another.

Earlier that morning I had read about trusting in the Lord with all my heart and not leaning on my own understanding (Prov. 3:5–7). That afternoon I received a telephone call that under normal circumstances would have caused me to feel anxious. But before I could hang up, God's still, small voice said to my heart, "Trust Me." That was all I needed. My spirit immediately relaxed, and I knew He was aware of my circumstances. He did not tell me what I needed to do for another week or so, but I had His Word tucked away in my heart. When I began to feel tempted or fearful, I would say, "Now, Lord, I'm trusting You. I don't know how all of this will work out, but I know You know. You have said, 'Trust Me,' and this is, what I'm going to do."

The voice of God brings peace. From the illustration above, you can understand how God's Word brings a sense of rest and contentment to our hearts. We can experience unbelievable difficulty, and with just a word from Him, our hearts become steady and our anxiety level drops. Most of us have heard of the person who did not believe in God but decided to pick up the Bible and begin reading it. When I hear about this, I usually think, *Deep down inside, that person wants to know God.* And I'm usually right; God's Word is sharper than any sword. It pierces our hearts with the truth of His unconditional love and acceptance. The moment we make a decision to read it, study it, and apply even a small portion of what we learn to our lives, we are changed. There is no way to read the Bible and remain lost and hardened by sin, doubt, and unbelief.

The lost person does not have true peace, which is God's peace living within him or her. This is the kind of peace that is not shaken by trial or difficulty. You may lose your job, home, and position in life, but if you know Jesus, you will have His peace—peace that surpasses all human understanding. Anxiety may threaten to rob your joy, depression may seek to steal your hope, but when you have God's Word hidden in the recesses of your heart and mind, peace will rule over every negative thought. Tragedy may strike, but you can rest in His omnipotent care.

CHAPTER 5

HIDE GOD'S WORD IN YOUR HEART

God stretches our faith and in doing so reveals our level of trust in Him. It also reveals how much we have learned about His ways. Do we really believe that He is in control of all things, or do we continue to feel as if we need to help Him work in times of difficulty? He watches to see how we will respond to our trying circumstances. Do we lean on His Word for answers to our problems, or do we rush to our own conclusions without consulting Him? One young man I was talking with spoke for a while about the pressure he was under at work. Suddenly, his countenance changed as he remembered how the Lord had encouraged him that morning. "I began my devotional time on the wrong foot," he admitted. "I was determined to list out the things that were going wrong and the bad attitudes others around me seemed to have. I was angry at the thought of having to deal with one more demand. Then I heard a loud noise outside my house and I got up to see what was wrong. There was nothing there, but as I got back on my knees, I sensed the Lord gently telling me that the 'noise' was reflective of the enemy's chatter in my mind. There was nothing for me to be concerned about because He was aware of my life and its direction. I just needed to trust Him."

He paused and said, "The thing that bothers me the most is how I actually tried not to believe what God was telling me. It was as if I wanted to get it all out. I wanted Him to hear my side of the story. Then I opened my Bible and began to read these words:

Lift up your eyes on high and see who has created these stars, the One who leads forth their host by number, He calls them all by name; because of the greatness of His might and the strength of His power, not one of them is missing.

Why do you say, O Jacob, and assert, O Israel, "My way is hidden from the LORD, and the justice due me escapes the notice of my God"? Do you not know? Have you not heard? The Everlasting God, the LORD, the Creator of the ends of the earth does not become weary or tired. His understanding is inscrutable. He gives strength to the weary, and to him who lacks might He increases power. Though youths grow weary and tired, and vigorous young men stumble badly, yet those who wait for the LORD will gain new strength; they will mount up with wings like eagles, they will run and not get tired, they will walk and not become weary. (Isa. 40:26–31)

"I asked God to forgive me," he continued, "because I realized He really was aware of my circumstances and had a plan even though He had not revealed it to me." When we are struggling and fighting against discouragement, God will speak to our hearts. This often includes the thought or memory of a familiar passage of Scripture. Learning to recall God's promises can assure that you will have the right encouragement when you need it the most.

A MATTER OF CHOICE

The Word of God protects us from evil because it refocuses our minds on the truth. But we can ignore it and suffer the consequences. God cannot force us to think on His precepts, but His Spirit will call out to us the way He did with this young man. He can call to us at any point. We may sense Him checking our spirits, cautioning us to be careful or not to make a certain decision. This is all well and good, but the greater impact comes when we take the time to study God's Word and allow Him to teach us His truth in Scripture. God's Word never fails.

If you want to draw near to Him, ask Him to teach you how to hide His Word in your heart. If you want the enemy to flee from you, taking his ruthless suggestions with him, begin to read and study God's Word. One of the Spirit's responsibilities is to protect and honor God's Word. Isaiah writes, "So is my word that goes out from my mouth: it will not return to me empty, but will accomplish what I desire and achieve the purpose for which I sent it" (55:11 NIV).

God speaks to us for a specific purpose. We never know what He has planned for our lives. The enemy may tell us that we can expect very little for our efforts, but the truth is, God has something wonderful coming our way. I often wonder how many believers quit right before the answer to their prayers is revealed. If you are in a difficult spot or battling discouragement, set your mind on one thing: staying the course. Run the race that He wants you to run and you will cross the finish line—you will receive a victor's crown. For the believer, winning the race begins long before you step into the starting blocks. It begins the moment you accept Christ as your Savior and open His Word and begin to read. Those who fail to do this may know that they are saved, but they miss knowing God in an intimate way.

RELATIONSHIP: THE MOST IMPORTANT PART

We will encounter difficulties in this life. There is no way to avoid them. We live in a fallen world. Tragedy strikes, sorrow builds, sin pulls at our hearts, and frustration will tempt us to throw in the towel and walk away from the very thing that God has called us to do. I want to challenge you not to follow that pattern. Instead, follow the pattern that God has given us in His Word—study His truth, ask Him to show you how to apply it to your life, and then hide it in your heart. Then, when discouragement comes, "Your ears will hear a word behind you, 'This is the way, walk in it,' whenever you turn to the right or to the left" (Isa. 30:21).

The psalmist prayed, "Let me hear Your lovingkindness in the morning; for I trust in You; teach me the way in which I should walk; for to You I lift up my soul" (143:8). The most important aspect of the Christian life is our personal relationship with Jesus Christ. God's overarching goal for our lives is not for us to be a success from an earthly standpoint. Success from His perspective is defined by our personal love for Him. Are we willing to dig deep in His Word so that we may know Him in an intimate way? Or do we just want to get by and pray only when trouble comes, hoping that He will hear our words? A relationship with Jesus Christ requires a commitment not only to God but also to the Savior and to His Word. He is the living Word of God. "In the beginning was the Word, and the Word was with God, and the Word was God" (John 1:1). If you want to know God, you must come to a point where you desire His fellowship, and this includes loving His Word. Once again, the words of the psalmist instruct us: "Consider how I love Your precepts; revive me, O LORD, according to Your lovingkindness" (119:159).

We worship and serve a God who is compassionate, loving, personal, and genuinely interested in everything that concerns us. He hears our cries, knows our needs, and is committed to answering our prayers, but we have a responsibility before Him. He speaks, but are we listening? And when we hear His voice and know His will, do we obey or dismiss it because we would rather continue on the path we have chosen to walk? This is a serious question. I have talked with people who know without a doubt what God wants them to do, but they hesitate, put it off, or simply disobey God.

King David knew God did not want him to number the people (2 Sam. 24). There was never a time in his reign when the Lord ordered him to consider how great his kingdom was. He was king over Israel; the Lord had fulfilled His promises, and yet something—some suggestion of pride—tempted David to check out the numbers, and God was not pleased. Far too often, people do not consider the consequences of disobedience, but the Bible teaches us how to do this. In fact, there are many benefits that come as a result of weaving God's Word into the fabric of your life. I've listed several below.

You will gain a sense of sureness. By this, I mean that you will have a strong sense that God is with you and that He is leading. In times of trial or when you make decisions, His Word is an anchor to your heart and mind. The psalmist writes, "From my distress I called upon the LORD; the LORD answered me and set me in a large place. The LORD is for me; I will not fear; what can man do to me? . . . It is better to take refuge in the LORD than to trust in man. It is better to take refuge in the LORD than to trust in princes" (118:5–6, 8–9). In Psalm 55:22, David writes, "Cast your burden upon the LORD and He will sustain you; He will never allow the righteous to be shaken." When you have God's Word in your heart, you have a powerful, priceless, eternal treasure and tool that cannot be duplicated by anything this world has to offer.

You will have fresh strength. You may be standing before a door of opportunity and blessing, but God has hidden it from your sight. The best way to renew your hope is to get alone with Him in prayer and read His Word. If you do not know where to begin, start with Psalms. Or even better than this, start with prayer, saying, "Lord, I need You to show me what to do. I don't know what is going on, but I feel frustrated, afraid, and even used. I don't mind being used by You, but I need to know that this is where You want me to be. Please reaffirm Your will to me through Your Word." There is no way that God will fail to answer this prayer. He will move heaven and earth to show you what you need to do and how you should respond to the situation.

You will have hope. I have had people tell me that there are times when they are frightened by what they read in God's Word. One nation totally wipes out another one or someone does something wrong and it seems that God punishes an entire group of people. But when we focus on the negative, we will not see or understand the faithfulness and goodness of God. Satan loves to take a portion of Scripture where someone has disobeyed the Lord and tell us that we are doing the same thing. Always remember, his goal is to divide our minds and turn us against God. The Bible is the greatest account of hope and faithfulness that has ever been written. We have hope regardless of our circumstances because He is our refuge and strength. Psalm 5:11–12 says, "Let all who take refuge in You be glad, let them ever sing for joy; and may You shelter them, that those who love Your name may exult in You. For it is You who blesses the righteous man, O Lord, You surround him with favor as with a shield." And the author of Proverbs writes, "Know that wisdom is thus for your soul; if you find it, then there will be a future, and your hope will not be cut off" (24:14).

You will experience joy and contentment. Happiness comes and goes, but when you know the truth of God, you can take a deep breath and relax. You have learned that there is nothing you can do on your own to receive salvation. You cannot work to achieve it. It is a free gift of God—a gift of grace that God offers you. It is not based on anything you have done. His gift of salvation is based on the sacrificial death of His Son on the cross. Your responsibility is to accept Him as your Savior and ask Him to forgive your sins. Believe in the gift He has given you and study about Him and His promises through reading His Word. As you do this, you will learn that God has a plan for your life. Contentment comes when you realize that you do not have to perform a certain way in order to receive God's love. No one cares for you as much as He does. Every need you have is His top priority and concern. He loves you, and He wants you to learn how to love and enjoy being in His presence—a holy, protective presence that offers shelter, encouragement, and infinite hope. Sorrows will come, but the love of God holds you close and will stand with you through every tearful moment.

You will have the peace of God covering your heart. When it does not seem that you can go on another day, He always finds a way to pour out His peace in your life. Sometimes this may come while you are reading His Word, but so often it comes when you are feeling fractured by others' demands or your own inability to cope with a life event. I remember years ago reading something Catherine Marshall wrote moments after her husband, Peter Marshall, died. She told how she sensed God's closeness as she looked down at Peter's earthly body. Then there was this simple but profound promise from God as she stood there: "Surely goodness and lovingkindness will follow *you* all the days of *your* life." The words were from Psalm 23 that she knew so well. God, however, had personalized them so they reflected His voice to her.

The promise was the same, and it was one that He never failed to meet. His abiding peace sustained her, not only in the aftermath of her husband's death, but through the years that she raised their son alone. Jesus said, "Peace I leave with you; My peace I give to you; not as the world gives do I give to you. Do not let your heart be troubled, nor let it be fearful" (John 14:27). Paul echoes these words: "Be anxious for nothing, but in everything by prayer and supplication with thanksgiving let your requests be made known to God. And the peace of God, which surpasses all comprehension, will guard your hearts and your minds in Christ Jesus" (Phil. 4:6–7).

Paul's words in Romans bring clarity to the reason many

people do not experience God's peace. He writes, "For the mind set on the flesh is death, but the mind set on the Spirit is life and peace, because the mind set on the flesh is hostile toward God" (8:6–7). Paul is addressing the person who does not know Christ, but he also is emphasizing the fact that when we become involved in the trappings of the world—its sinful attitudes and pleasure— we can expect to feel anxious, frustrated, and confused.

Entertainment is probably one of the greatest problem areas a believer will face. I cannot begin to tell you the number of people who, over the years, have talked with me about the television programs and movies they have watched. One woman, who was determined to watch a certain program each day that portrayed adultery as a normal part of life, could not understand why she fought feelings of lust. She told me, "I have the Spirit of God living within me! He is stronger than the things of this world!" My reply was, "Yes, and He is telling you to stop subjecting Him to displays of sin." People get into so many hurtful and wrong situations as a result of willfully disengaging from God's holiness. They wonder why they lie awake at night with their minds running from one negative thought to another. When your mind is focused on earthly pleasures, sins, pressures, and demands instead of the faithfulness of God, you will feel restless and as if something is not quite right. You won't be able to settle down because there will be a sincere lack of peace. How do you gain God's peace for your life?

- Read His Word
- Study His Word
- Apply it to your life
- Ask Him to show you how to believe and trust all that you have read

The consequences of sin are obvious: restlessness, a lack of peace, an absence of sustaining faith, feelings of anxiety, a sense of confusion, and doubt. I cannot think of a single problem God has failed to answer in His Word. The Bible is His instruction book—from cover to cover. If I want Him to speak to me through Scripture, then His Word must be in my heart and mind. It has to be available in a place where the Spirit can easily retrieve it and remind me of God's truth. If it is hidden in my heart, then when I turn on the television and something starts rolling across the screen, then I will know that what I am doing or seeing does not fit who I am in Christ. It is not peace producing but is worldly attractive, and that always leads to feelings opposite those that God wants us to experience.

When we fail to obey God by not reading His Word, we miss His best. We don't have the guidance we need, the encouragement we long to have, or the sense of joy, peace, and contentment that He wants to give us. It is like we have been placed on a major league sports team but we have refused to learn how to catch the ball or swing the bat. We have no idea what a goal or a touchdown is. We show up for the game, but within moments of the start, we are knocked down, struck out, and carried off the field. We never picked up the instruction book, and consequently we are clueless about what we need to do. This does not have to be reflective of your life. Hide His Word in your heart and you will have the wisdom you need for every situation in life. "For the LORD gives wisdom; from His mouth come knowledge and understanding. He stores up sound wisdom for the upright; He is a shield to those who walk in integrity" (Prov. 2:6–7).

CHAPTER 6

OPEN YOUR HEART TO GOD'S TRUTH

When God speaks to us, He always has something very specific to say. He never speaks in generalities. His words are full of love and understanding. He may be direct and firm, but He is never belittling or confusing. And He is always encouraging and reassures us of His devotion. I have found that no matter when God speaks to me, He is always guiding and directing me in a certain way. Sometimes He may speak to our hearts with the idea of letting us know that He is aware of our circumstances. Or He may just want to tell us that He loves us and remind us that He has a plan for our lives. Someone reading these words may think, *I'm too old for God to have a plan for my life.* But you are never too old or too young to used by God.

When Jesus was a baby in His mother's arms, God used Him to confirm the promise He had given to Simeon and Anna years earlier. When Joseph and Mary brought Jesus to the temple to dedicate Him on the eighth day after His birth, they saw these dear saints of God in the temple. Most of their lives had been spent waiting for the Messiah to come. And suddenly He was there; He was just a baby, but they recognized Him. Age was not a prohibitive factor to God, and it should not be to you either. He can use anyone whose heart is turned toward Him in love and devotion. You may say, "But you don't know what I have done in the past." I don't have to know because God knows and He loves you with an eternal love. When you ask for His forgiveness, He forgives and He also cleanses you from all unrighteousness (1 John 1:7, 9). You may feel hopeless at times. But feelings have nothing to do with the truth of God's Word. When you give your life to Christ, He will make something wonderful out of it. How does He do this? He changes you from the inside out. He teaches you to desire His goodness, love, and mercy rather than the things of this world.

What Is God's Goal?

The closer you come to Him, the more you will desire to know Him, and the more you know about Him, the more you will desire to do His will. God wants us to want to know Him. James writes, "Draw near to God and He will draw near to you" (4:8). This is the call of His Word to You: "Come to Me, and learn of Me." In Matthew, Jesus says, "Come to Me, all who are weary and heavy-laden, and I will give you rest. Take My yoke upon you and learn from Me, for I am gentle and humble in heart, and you will find rest for your souls. For My yoke is easy and My burden is light"

(11:28–30). God will renew your mind and direct your steps so that your life honors Him. When He is honored, you will enjoy unspeakable blessings. Over the years I have noticed that many people have a hard time making a commitment to Christ. Paul offers us this word of caution:

> Let no one deceive you with empty words, for because of these things the wrath of God comes upon the sons of disobedience. Therefore do not be partakers with them; for you were formerly darkness, but now you are Light in the Lord; walk as children of Light (for the fruit of the Light consists in all goodness and righteousness and truth), trying to learn what is pleasing to the Lord. Do not participate in the unfruitful deeds of darkness, but instead even expose them; for it is disgraceful even to speak of the things which are done by them in secret. But all things become visible when they are exposed by the light, for everything that becomes visible is light. For this reason it says, "Awake, sleeper, and arise from the dead, and Christ will shine on you."
>
> Therefore be careful how you walk, not as unwise men but as wise, making the most of your time, because the days are evil. (Eph. 5:6–16)

We do not know when Christ will return; therefore we need to live each day as if His coming is imminent.

Paul understood that God had set him aside for a specific purpose before the moment of his birth. The same was true of His Son and of us as well. God has predestined us to be conformed to His image (Rom. 8:29). This means He has drawn a circle around our lives. He knows the plans He has for us (Jer. 29:11). We can short-circuit this through deliberate ignorance or disobedience, or we can heed His warnings and directions.

When I was a teenager, an incident occurred that was a startling example of God's intervention in my life. One day after taking a shower, I realized I had left the light on in the bathroom and went back in to turn it off. I was still barefoot and the floor was very damp. Just before I reached up to pull the metal cord hanging above my head, the telephone rang. Instead of going ahead and pulling the chain, I chose to answer the phone. But when I said, "Hello," there was no reply. No one was on the line. Not thinking much of it, I turned and walked back to the bathroom. But before I went through the doorway, I stopped and was stunned by what I saw—a light fixture with a metal cord hanging down and a puddle of water directly below it. If I had reached up and pulled the chain, I could have died instantly; the bathroom could have become my electric chair. That is how close I was to death. I had heard people talk about how God works in our lives, but up until that moment, I don't think I remember giving it a very serious thought. Suddenly I became aware that He was aware of me. I remember praying, "Lord, You have just saved my life. No one was on the phone—only You."

Before this experience, I had tried to read my Bible, but I didn't know how. Now I knew He loved me and had a purpose for my life.

We have a limited free will (limited because ultimately only God is sovereign over all things). We can choose to do something other than commit our lives to Him. I could have ignored the telephone that day, but something within me urged me to leave where I was standing and answer it. God won't force us to study His Word, or demand a commitment, but we are the ones who miss a great blessing. When I returned and saw what could have been my end, I knew I had to learn more about God— Someone who loved me so much that He diverted my attention and saved my life. To know Him and love Him was His will for my life.

People often come to me with problems that in the beginning could have been solved so simply. But they kept pushing and going forward without taking time to consult the one Person who really has the answer they need. They make one wrong decision after another until they are standing at a dead end. Their lives bear the evidence of suffering, shame, and disappointment. They have the choice to either shut God out of their lives or seize the opportunity to hear His voice and obey. I have also found that many people do not want to spend the effort to know God. They want the benefits of having a relationship with Him, but they do not want to get serious about their relationship with Him.

They go to church, serve on committees, and participate in

church-related programs, but when it comes to actually knowing God—His truth and principles—they look for the first side door and leave. Then, when life becomes difficult, they do not have the tools they need to deal with the situation. Or if they have the opportunity to make a life-changing decision, they stumble in fear—worrying and wondering if they are doing the right thing. Limited knowledge about who God is and His personal love for each one of us limits our ability to live the Christian life. We can't make a clear, wise decision apart from God's Word. We can make a decision and it may turn out to be okay, but we will wonder, *Have I done the right thing? Is this the best choice?* If you have spent time with God in prayer and studying His Word, you will know the right way to go.

The apostle Paul came to an understanding that God had called him to preach the gospel. He also had a clear understanding as to who was doing the teaching. Once we understand that it is God who is calling to us, we have a serious decision to make. Either we answer Him with yes, or we try to sidestep His will and plan and suffer the consequences. It is God's goal for each one of us to know Him. He doesn't want a casual "Hi, how are You, God?" He is looking for a full commitment. This is what He found in Paul's life. Paul writes, "When God, who had set me apart even from my mother's womb and called me through His grace, was pleased to reveal His Son in me so that I might preach Him among the Gentiles, I did not immediately consult with flesh and blood, nor did I go up to

Jerusalem to those who were apostles before me; but I went away to Arabia, and returned once more to Damascus" (Gal. 1:15–17).

Paul understood God's truth concerning his life. And *the first goal* that God has for you and me is to comprehend the truth. He wants us to understand His principles. Paul, through personal study and prayer, realized that God was calling Him to preach the gospel to as many people as possible. Still, he did not run to one place after another. He was led by God's Spirit into Arabia, where He personally trained him. Only later did the Spirit allow him to go to Jerusalem, where he met Peter, James, and the others. He wants to do the same thing in your life—lead you to a spiritual Arabia where you can grasp His truth and understand His ways.

The second goal God has for us is to realize that His Word is progressive. You cannot read one book and think you know what the entire Bible teaches. The entire book is the revelation of God because it is drawn from His mind. Even Jesus said, "For I did not speak on My own initiative, but the Father Himself who sent Me has given Me a commandment as to what to say and what to speak" (John 12:49). God's Word is alive (Heb. 4:12). You may read a passage of Scripture and think you understand it perfectly, but when you come back to it a few months later under different circumstances, you suddenly understand an entirely new truth. God's principles do not change, but because they are so relative to our lives and the circumstances we experience, we can study

His Word for a lifetime and still enjoy it as being new, exciting, and infinitely insightful.

Read the Major and Minor Prophets, and you will learn more. Meditate on the Psalms, and you will gain even more wisdom as you read Proverbs. Study the Gospels, and Paul's writings will come alive in your mind. Read the first five books of the Bible or Revelation, and you will be stunned by the wonder of God's awesome power. There is nothing boring about God's Word and certainly there is nothing that brings more peace, joy, and hope than His Word to us through the unshakable, undeniable truth of an infinite, loving God who has set His affections on us. When you open yourself up to the study of God's Word and begin to read a little bit, then you will want to read more.

Each time you read the Bible, you are gaining deeper knowledge about God Himself and about the world He has created. The more we want to serve Him, the more we will give to others. Andrew loved to bring people to Jesus. He knew the Savior, and he wanted others to know Him too. It didn't matter whether it was a grown man or woman or a young boy with five barley loaves and two fish, Andrew wanted to introduce people to Jesus (John 6:8). He knew if people met the Savior, their lives would be changed. Can you imagine what the young boy felt as he watched and listened to the disciples debate about what to do with his lunch?

Jesus knew exactly what was going to happen. He was the One who was going to do it, and the young boy was going to witness a great miracle. It was a life-changing opportunity to be present as Jesus blessed and multiplied the bread and the fish so there was enough to feed five thousand people. Moments like this one are not restricted to the New Testament. God continues to demonstrate His power to save, provide, heal, and restore those who come to Him. Jesus Christ is absolutely sufficient for every need we have and for every circumstance we encounter. But how do you know any of this if you do not pick up His Word and read what He wants to say to you? He wants us to discover the truth about His majesty, power, love, grace, and other attributes.

He also wants us to understand the truth about ourselves—that we are inadequate and sinful. One woman who was called to be a missionary prayed often, "Lord, not by my strength because I am not adequate for the task." Her words were not a display of low self-esteem but rather, like the apostle Paul, an acknowledgment of her need for God's strength in times of weakness. "Therefore I am well content with weaknesses, with insults, with distresses, with persecutions, with difficulties, for Christ's sake; for when I am weak, then I am strong" (2 Cor. 12:10).

Understanding your position as a child of God is very important, especially when reading and studying God's Word. If we view ourselves as people whose lives do not count for much, we will feel overlooked, ignored, and forgotten. We will tend to have a negative outlook when it comes to the things of God. Satan encourages this thought. He wants you and me to feel isolated because He knows if we focus on our feelings, then we will begin to act as if they are true. And they are not! The enemy tries to tell us that God is unhappy with us, wants to punish us, and does not have a plan for our futures. But he knows the opposite is true. Paul reminds us of the extreme potential we have as children of God. He writes, "I can do all things through Him who strengthens me" (Phil. 4:13). If you have never accepted Christ as your Savior, you do not have the same advantage. You are right: you have to "go it alone," carve out your own way in life, fight to get ahead of everyone else, and make sure no one overlooks your many abilities.

Those whose lives are hidden in Christ know the power that comes from leaning on Him, allowing Him to guide them, and trusting Him to take care of them at every turn in life. Do you know this for your own life? Have you experienced the peace that comes when you wake up in the middle of the night and things start rushing through your mind begging for attention? If you have taken time to read and study God's Word, then turn to your bedside, pick up your Bible, and find comfort for every thought. You also will know what is true and what is Satan's attempt to tempt you to be anxious over the very things that God has commanded us not to fear.

Reading His Word, hiding His truth in our hearts, and listening for His instruction are essential for our prosperity and success. If we choose to ignore, dismiss, or shun the Bible, we are setting ourselves up for failure. Even if we do achieve some degree of success, without a strong foundation based on the Word of God, we will be blown apart much like the home mentioned in the introduction of this book. The storms will come, and if we have not built our *lives* on the rock of God's truth, they will come crashing down—physically, emotionally, mentally, and spiritually. Those who do not know Christ are lost. They think they are on the right road, but what they don't realize is that the road they are on leads only to one destination: destruction. But God had a formula for success and He gave it to Joshua: "Do not become afraid because I AM with you and do not let My Word pass out of your memory. Meditate on it, study it, and then you will always know what is right to do."

One of the wonderful things about God is that He knows we need His encouragement and His grace to provide it. After the nation had crossed the Jordan River and was preparing to march against Jericho, the Lord appeared to Joshua:

Now it came about when Joshua was by Jericho, that he lifted up his eyes and looked, and behold, a man was standing opposite him with his sword drawn in his hand, and Joshua went to him and said to him "Are you for us or for our adversaries?" He said, "No; rather I indeed come now as captain of the host of the LORD." And Joshua fell on his face to the earth, and bowed down, and said to him, "What has my lord to say to his servant?" The captain of the LORD'S host said to Joshua, "Remove your sandals from your feet, for the place where you are standing is holy." And Joshua did so. (Josh. 5:13–15)

God always speaks to us when we need Him the most. The night before the battle when many of the others were asleep, Joshua was awake going over the details God had given him. What an awesome reminder of His personal care for His servant! He sent His angel—theologians believe it was the Lord Jesus Christ—to encourage him. You may think, *I wish God would do this for me.* He wants to do this very thing, and He does do it for all who listen for His coming. He has given us His Word and His Spirit. We don't have to look for a mighty warrior to appear; we have the battle plan, the call to arms, and the victory manual with us. Not only this, we have the Holy Spirit—God's infinite presence with us—to champion our cause and grant us victory and hope. Why do we doubt?

Jesus asked Peter this very question, "You of little faith, why did you doubt?" (Matt. 14:31). It was the fourth watch of the night when Jesus came to His disciples in the midst of a raging storm. At first they thought He was a ghost, but after hearing His voice, they realized it was Jesus. Peter was so bold as to call out to Him, "Lord, if it is You, command me to come to You on the water" (v. 28). He had learned that a command given by Jesus contained immense power. Therefore he stepped out onto the raging sea and began walking to Jesus. We know what happened next. Peter's faith waned when he saw the size of the waves and felt the power of the wind against him. God always brings us back to a point where we are totally dependent on Him. This is what He did in Joshua's life and it is certainly what He did concerning Peter. He wants us to understand:

- Who He is—absolute holiness
- Who we are—His beloved children created in His likeness
- The knowledge that is available to us through His Word

How to Listen to the Voice of God

When preaching, I have found there are two kinds of listeners. The first kind are passive and nonchalant—people who can "take it or leave it" when it comes to the Bible. Then there are those who are aggressive listeners. These people have a look of hunger on their faces. They attend church to learn more about God and to worship Him. They are not there to hear a pastor speak. Instead, they are present to hear from God. There is a huge difference. An aggressive listener wants to hear truth even when it may be painful to assimilate. He hungers for righteousness and thirsts to know more about the ways of God, and he yearns to find out the answers to his questions by probing and studying the Bible. People who are aggressive listeners will take notes, reread them during the week, and ask God to show them how what they have heard applies to their lives. They are not afraid to become involved with the active study of His Word. They want to know the truth because they have learned a great secret—the more they know about God, the more peace, contentment, hope, joy, and blessing they experience. If you read and study His Word, He will bless you. "Blessed is he who reads and those who hear the words of the prophecy, and heed the things which are written in it; for the time is near" (Rev. 1:3). God wants you to be an aggressive listener of His Word because He wants you to be able to comprehend the truth. He knows if you do this, your life will be radically changed for Him.

What are His goals for you in reading and listening to His Word?

He wants you to understand His truth so you can apply it to your life.

He wants you to be transformed by what you read, study, and hear. Remember what we read earlier in Isaiah? "So is my word that goes out from my mouth: it will not return to me empty, but will accomplish what I desire and achieve the purpose for which I sent it" (55:11 NIV). God not only has a purpose for your life, He has a purpose for the words He speaks to you. I mentioned earlier that there have been times in my life when the only two words I heard from the Lord were, "Trust Me." And I was committed to do just that—trust Him even though I did not know where He was leading me or what I would do. He knew, He is sovereign, and He has promised to love me forever. How could I doubt His ability and goodness? And yet, when trials come or situations take a course other than the one we have planned, we suddenly find ourselves crying out like Peter, "Lord, save me!" It is times like this that we should turn to His Word, because it will transform us and remove our doubts and fears. It teaches us how to trust Him even when the way before us appears to be a dead end. He opened the Red Sea for the nation of Israel, and He will do the same for you when you need to pass through to a place of safety.

Week after week, as you are in His Word, He is putting Scripture into your heart and He is molding and shaping your life for something absolutely wonderful. You can trust this: the time you spend learning His truths will not be wasted. He is planning to use you in ways you never dreamed possible, but first you must be trained by His Word. When you and I begin to comprehend the truth and allow God to conform us to that truth, then our lives will take on an undeniable likeness to Jesus Christ, and we gain all the benefit of knowing God and seeing Him work in and through us. When problems come, we know how to stop and think through them by asking the Lord to show us how to respond. We are not reacting any more; we are responding according to what we have learned from God.

Remember the story of Mary and Martha in Luke 10:38–42?

Is there any doubt as to why Mary was sitting at the feet of Jesus? She truly had learned what was most important—the Word of God—and she chose to spend time listening to Him instead of busying herself with the things of the world. What is most important to you? To be seen, noticed, or stroked for your professional ability, or to know that you are loved and cared for by an awesome loving God who has you in the center of His will and affections? This is one of the occasions when God allows you to decide: you can resist Him and His Word, or you can receive Him and the truth He wants to pour into your life. If you accept His invitation to come, He will give you His peace to stand guard over your life.

He wants to communicate with you. I find this one fact very humbling. To think the God of the universe wants to know me, speak to me, and help me understand how to live is more than I can comprehend. He knew Joshua was struggling, and instead of just sending some simple word of encouragement, He came Himself and reminded young Joshua that there was no need to be afraid because he was not alone. The absolute Ruler of everything was with him, and he was not going to fail. When our hearts are weary and we want to give up, His Word of encouragement gives us the strength to go beyond what we believe we can do. Joshua had no idea how he would lead Israel, but God knew and He had promised to guide him. "Do not tremble or be dismayed, for the LORD your God is with you wherever you go"

(Josh. 1:9). Wherever you go, God is with you—watching over you, protecting you, and providing the truth you need for every situation. The question is, will you open your heart to His Word, apply it to your life, and allow God to change you so that He can use you in ways far greater than you can imagine?

CHAPTER 7

APPLY GOD'S PROMISES TO YOUR LIFE

I remember where I was and the exact time when God gave me a very important promise. I had been up for a while praying as I normally do in the mornings when I decided I needed to get ready for an appointment. It was eight o'clock and I was in Kansas City. As I walked past a bay window that overlooked the rooftops of nearby buildings, I stopped to enjoy the view for a moment. Then without warning, I sensed God speaking to me. It was as if He said, "Here is what I'm going to do." He didn't ask me to comment or what I thought about what He had said. He just spoke directly to my spirit, and I was immediately humbled by what I heard. His words addressed the future of In Touch Ministries and in particular how we would continue to spread the gospel message around the world. As I backed away from the window, I asked, "How, Lord?" Then I stepped back up to the window and looked to my left. I saw several buildings that were outfitted with satellite disks. "That is how I'm going to do it," I sensed Him say.

Today, the In Touch program is broadcast all over the world. Without a doubt, God fulfilled His promise to me and He is still fulfilling it. That morning my heart was open to what He wanted to say to me. I had laid aside my personal wants and only had Him as my focus. God's promises are not mystical or reserved for one person over another. They are in His Word, and they are available to everyone who seeks Him. But you must be willing to do whatever He leads you to do. Many people have heard this story and responded by saying, "I wish I could hear from God. He never speaks to me." But He is speaking to you, and He wants to tell you all about Himself and the dreams, goals, and desires He has for you. The greater question is, are you still enough to hear Him?

Another factor is that while He is willing to speak to your heart and mind, you must be open to hearing His voice. This means you must be willing to submit and obey. No matter who you are, if you are intent on pushing your agenda, looking to have your needs met, and are only worried about yourself, chances are you won't be able to hear from God. He may be talking, but you won't hear Him because your only focus is yourself. God's greatest desire is for you to long to know Him. He wants you to experience His unconditional love and care, but He also wants you to learn how to trust Him and to desire to know Him personally and intimately. Receiving a promise from God is not difficult, but it does require a surrendered heart whose only desires are to love, worship, and please the Lord. Learning how to study, claim, and apply His promises to your life is crucial to your spiritual growth and Christian walk because the process involves submission and commitment to God.

Over the years I have heard people praying for all kinds of things that they really did not need. I'm not saying that God is opposed to giving us the things we need. He promises to meet every need according to His riches—and He is very wealthy (Phil. 4:19). He also gives you many of the desires of your heart. After all, there are times when He plants desires in your heart for a specific purpose—to bless you. This means there is nothing wrong with driving a nice car, owning a new home, dressing nicely, or placing your children in good schools.

The problem comes when we fail to see Him for who He is—awesome in nature, worthy of all praise, and the only source of our worship. When priorities get out of line, you may find yourself looking at what others have and feeling envious. Then, when you do sit down to study the Bible or pray, your mind is full of clutter—thoughts that have no place in the life of a believer. You may actually need something that God wants to give you, but because you are stuck in a negative gear—complaining about what you don't have—you can't see or appreciate what He already has given you.

Learning how to claim the promises of God requires a godly perspective. It also requires patience because there will be times when He gives us a promise but we do not see it materialize for a long time. Consider the promises He made to Joseph and David along with the Major and Minor Prophets. Sometimes it was years and even generations before these people saw the promises of God come to pass. In fact, the author of Hebrews provides a list of people who were waiting for the promise of God to be fulfilled by the coming of the Messiah but died without seeing Him, yet this did not change their faith in God. They knew He was faithful, and at the right time—at the right moment—the Messiah would come, and He did.

We may go a very long time without hearing a word from Him spoken to our hearts. Yet we can study our Bibles, learn His principles, and continue to grow in our walk with Him because we know that He is aware of every breath we take. Nothing escapes His sight. We have a sense of peace because we know He has promised never to forsake us. He tells us in Hebrews, "Make sure that your character is free from the love of money, being content with what you have; for He Himself has said, 'I will never desert you, nor will I ever forsake you,' so that we confidently say, 'The Lord is my helper, I will not be afraid'" (13:5–6). Promises like this and countless others are ones we can claim knowing they will never fail. There may be seasons when we do not hear a firm word from Him. But even then, we have His Word as a light to our paths. And if we never hear His voice again in our hearts and minds, we still have His spoken Word given to us by the Holy Spirit to read, study, and apply. The truth is, God is always speaking to us in some way, but we must be still enough to hear and recognize His voice over the endless chatter of the world and of Satan.

APPROPRIATING GOD'S PROMISES

Peter writes, "He has granted to us His precious and magnificent promises, so that by them you may become partakers of the divine nature" (2 Pet. 1:4). God's promises are precious, magnificent, and have extreme value. The author of Hebrews admonishes us with these words: "Do not throw away your confidence, which has a great reward. For you have need of endurance, so that when you have done the will of God, you may receive what was promised" (10:35–36). Notice he says, "When you have done the will of God." Promises are not given without a plan that involves faith and responsibility, though many times we have to wait for them to be revealed. A biblical promise is a declaration of God's intention to graciously bestow a gift upon an individual or a group of people. For example, Jesus said, "In My Father's house are many dwelling places; if it were not so, I would have told you; for I go to prepare a place for you. If I go and prepare a place for you, I will come again and receive you to Myself, that where I am, there you may be also" (John 14:2–3). He knows that at times we may feel tempted to wonder if He is really coming back for us, and so

He gives us the promise of His sure return and also of His personal care to reassure us and calm our fears.

In 1 Kings, we read where Solomon has been praying. In fact, he has been blessing the Lord for His faithfulness. Then he makes this statement: "Blessed be the LORD, who has given rest to His people Israel, according to all that He promised; not one word has failed of all His good promise, which He promised through Moses His servant" (8:56). God did exactly what He had promised to do, and Solomon was honoring the Lord by acknowledging it. He had a grateful heart, and he wanted the people to respond in gratitude also. How many times have you prayed for something, asking God to meet a need that you have and to speak to you through His Word, and as you read the Bible, He provided assurance that He heard your prayers and will answer? This is a tremendous gift. But instead of turning to Him with a grateful heart, did you pick up the telephone and call three or four people to tell them the news? So often we forget to thank the One person who provides the resources we need. I believe God's heart must hurt over our self-centered actions. We pray and trust Him and then forget to say, "Lord, thank You for answering my prayers. Thank You for being faithful to the promise You gave me in Your Word. Thank You for meeting my needs perfectly and on time."

Even those who encountered Jesus during His time here on earth neglected to thank Him:

While [Jesus] was on the way to Jerusalem, He was passing between Samaria and Galilee. As He entered a village, ten leprous men who stood at a distance met Him; and they raised their voices, saying, "Jesus, Master, have mercy on us!" When He saw them, He said to them, "Go and show yourselves to the priests." And as they were going, they were cleansed. Now one of them, when he saw that he had been healed, turned back, glorifying God with a loud voice, and he fell on his face at His feet, giving thanks to Him. And he was a Samaritan. Then Jesus answered and said, "Were there not ten cleansed? But the nine—where are they?" (Luke 17:11–17)

Nine of these men met the Savior-Healer (Ps. 103:3), but they never thought to thank God or worship Him for His healing. Hebrews 10:23 reminds us to "hold fast the confession of our hope without wavering, for He who promised is faithful." God is not going to give you a promise and then say, "You know, maybe I didn't mean that." And when He does answer, He wants us to give Him glory and praise because He truly has worked on our behalf.

When He gives us a promise, we can be sure He will do what He has said. It is a matter of demonstrating His character and nature to us. Believing God, trusting God, studying His Word, and applying it to your life are elements of the Christian faith that must work together. God is not going to operate one way one day and then another way the next. What He tells us in His Word will always line up with His nature and character. God is faithful. Therefore His Word is trustworthy and His promises are too. He is faithful to keep every one. Not one promise will fail—ever. People will say one thing and then go and do something else. Many will be kind and supportive in your presence but later will oppose you. But God never will. He is the same yesterday, today, and forever (Heb. 13:8). That is a promise you can claim! Why does God choose to give promises to you and me?

He wants us to learn something about His character. God is faithful, true, loving, patient, forgiving, kind, and so much more. He gives promises to us so that we will see His nature and learn deeper truths about His character and personal care for us.

You may have a definite need and wonder what God is going to do. You have prayed and asked Him to give you His wisdom. While studying His Word, you find yourself reading the following: "Trust in the LORD with all your heart and do not lean on your own understanding. In all your ways acknowledge Him, and He will make your paths straight" (Prov. 3:5–6). Is this a promise you can claim? Absolutely. God is saying, "I'm aware of what you are facing. I know your need. Trust Me, lean on Me and not on your human knowledge, and I will provide all that you need and so much more." Paul underscores this very thing when he writes, "My God will supply all your needs according to His riches in glory in Christ Jesus" (Phil. 4:19). In 1 Thessalonians, he simply tells us, "Faithful is He who calls you, and He also will bring it to pass" (5:24). God is honored and glorified when we trust Him and when we pray, "Lord, show me in Your Word a promise that I can cling to in this trying time." There is not a time when God refuses to answer the prayers of His people. He says call to Me and I will hear your voice (Jer. 33:3).

He wants to give us hope. All of us are encouraged when we know that someone is pulling for us—someone who wants us to cross the finish line victoriously. You may be able to think of a time when you did not know whether you were doing the right thing or not. Then someone you admired walked up to you and said, "God has placed you on my heart, and I want you to know that I'm praying for you." God wants you to know that He cares for you. He is cheering for you, and He has a plan for your life. Psalm 62:1–2 says, "My soul waits in silence for God only; from Him is my salvation. He only is my rock and my salvation, my stronghold; I shall not be greatly shaken." And Psalm 18:33–36 promises, "He makes my feet like hinds' feet, and sets me upon my high places. He trains my hands for battle, so that my arms can bend a bow of bronze. You have also given me the shield of Your salvation, and Your right hand upholds me; and Your gentleness makes me great. You enlarge my steps under me, and my feet have not slipped."

God is faithful to keep each and every promise. He is all-powerful, and we can trust Him to take care of all that concerns us. The prophet Isaiah emphasizes His power and majesty: "Lift up your eyes on high and see who has created these stars, the One who leads forth their host by number, He calls them all by name; because of the greatness of His might and the strength of His power, not one of them is missing" (40:26). Not only does God take care of the heavens, He personally watches over you and me. Why do people doubt God's ability? Usually we fail to trust God because we don't want to lose control over our lives or our circumstances. This is almost laughable because the God of the universe—the same God who created you and me and who has numbered the stars in the sky and holds each one in its place—certainly has the ability to take care of my life and my problems.

In Lamentations, Jeremiah writes, "This I recall to my mind, therefore I have hope. The LORD's lovingkindnesses indeed never cease, for His compassions never fail. They are new every morning; great is Your faithfulness. 'The LORD is my portion,' says my soul, 'therefore I have hope in Him'" (3:21–24). No matter what your circumstance, God's Word has a promise of hope waiting for you. You can try to figure out a way to encourage yourself, or you can say with the psalmist, "But as for me, I will hope continually, and will praise You yet more and more" (71:14).

He wants to develop our faith in Him. When we begin to trust God for simple answers to prayer, our faith increases. The more we read and study His Word, the more aware we become of His ability. One lesson learned at the feet of God builds on another until we have come to a point where we are talking through every decision we need to make with Him. We also discover that if we ask Him to show us what we should do, He does it! He speaks to us through His Word. Then, when we meditate on Scripture, we begin to internalize His truth in our hearts. From this point, we express our needs and God responds by giving us insight and wisdom. He also promises to move in certain ways and provide for the needs we have.

One young woman told me how God had led her back to college. It was a walk of faith because she was an older student and her parents did not have the means to support her financially. She received grants and worked throughout her years in college. During the second semester of her freshman year, she ran out of money completely. She had to register for classes and knew that once she signed the papers, college officials would want to know how she was going to pay for her classes. Whenever she prayed about it, God brought two passages of Scripture to mind: Jeremiah 29:11 and 1 Thessalonians 5:24. Both speak of God's faithfulness. As she waited in line to register for her classes, she kept thinking through her decision to return to college and how God had opened one door after another. Each time He had led her on to the next step.

She knew she could trust Him to fulfill His promises to her, and He did just that. College officials informed her that she had received not only two grants but also a scholarship that covered any remaining tuition with plenty left over to cover payment for all her books for her classes. Whatever God calls us to do, He will confirm it in His Word and He also will provide all that we need to accomplish the task. This is how our faith is built. He opens a door and we step through it. He opens another one, and once again we trust Him because we have learned that He is faithful, not some of the time, but all of the time!

There is a tremendous danger in opening God's Word and searching for a verse of Scripture to justify what we want to do. The difference between actually receiving a promise from God and searching for one that we believe fits our scenario is obvious. First, the Lord expects us to come to Him as children seeking His guidance and not looking for a word to justify our desires. When our lives are submitted to Him, we will pray and acknowledge our needs to Him, and then we will ask Him to lead us to a promise we can claim that will encourage, guide, and teach us what we need to do. This is how we can live godly lives that overflow with thanksgiving and praise. We have a sure hope and that is Jesus Christ. He is our advocate before the Father. Whatever concerns us concerns Him.

CONDITIONAL VERSUS UNCONDITIONAL PROMISES

I have had people ask me if all the promises in the Bible could be claimed today. The answer is no. There are specific promises that God gave certain people and the nation of Israel that are not ones we can claim for our lives. One example of this is the promise God gave Abraham and Sarah concerning the birth of Isaac. "'I will surely return to you at this time next year; and behold, Sarah your wife will have a son.' . . . Now Abraham and Sarah were old, advanced in age; Sarah was past childbearing. Sarah laughed to herself, saying, 'After I have become old, shall I have pleasure, my lord being old also?' . . . 'Is anything too difficult for the LORD? At the appointed time I will return to you, at this time next year, and Sarah will have a son'" (Gen. 18:10–12, 14). This was a promise that God gave these two people. We can't claim it or one like it for ourselves, but we can learn from the way they trusted God. We also can apply the truth that God said to them: "Is anything too difficult for the LORD?" I have been in a situation when I have thought, *Lord, I don't know how You are going to work all of this out, but I'm going to trust You.* It may have been one of the hardest things I had to do, but I held fast to my faith and allowed God to demonstrate His ability, especially in light of His promises to me. He has never failed me, and I have found His Word to be truth for every situation; nothing is too difficult for Him. And it won't be too hard for you if you have placed your trust in Him, taken time to study His Word and promises, and then chosen to go forward by faith believing that He will open a way before you.

Many of God's promises are conditional. They are based on a commandment that He has given us. He has instructed us to tithe our income—not because He needs our money, but because He wants to bless us. However, if we fail to obey Him, then we miss the blessing and the gift of His provisions. We may get by, but we won't experience the fullness of joy and goodness and surprise that He wants to send our way. I could list several of God's conditional promises. For example, "Confess that Jesus Christ is Lord and you will be saved." What is the condition of this promise? It is confession that Christ is our Savior and Lord.

Trust in the Lord with all your heart and He will guide your steps. The condition for this promise is one of trust—we must trust God to receive guidance. In Hebrews 11, we read, "Without faith it is impossible to please [God], for he who comes to God must believe He is a rewarder of those who seek Him" (v. 6). Most of God's promises are conditional—this means they are fulfilled as we obey God by faith through some action. He promised to heal us from all our diseases (Ps. 103:3), but we must believe in Him. And many times, His healing or His answer may not be what we want or expect. But in Psalm 68:19, God promises to "daily bear our burden." This is an unconditional promise because He is our burden bearer. It is unconditional because He does not say, "I will bear your burden, if you respond this way." No, it is a promise because it is His nature to bear the weight of the world's problems. Jesus bore our sins. He is our Savior. We must trust in Him to receive the fullness of this promise, but it does not change who He is—the

Savior, the Son of God, our Redeemer, and the King of kings and the Lord of lords.

IS THIS PROMISE FROM YOU, LORD?

There are several ways you can evaluate a promise to find out if it is God's promise for you or something that you have developed on your own. Let's say you are having serious car trouble. You need a reliable car to get you to work or to pick up children from school. After praying and laying the entire matter before God, you ask Him to give you a promise in His Word that will help you make a wise decision. You start off with a modest estimate of what you would like to spend, but before you know it, your mind is off and running: *A sunroof would be nice,* you think. *Something with extra room would be great. Then I could carry my son's soccer gear and all of his friends to practice. New! I would love a new car straight off the showroom floor or lot or whatever as long as it is new so I won't have to worry about having car trouble for a long time.*

God knows your needs, and He may have this for you and much more. But the greatest excitement comes when we don't try to "super size" God and instead ask Him to give us the desire of our hearts but also to make sure that they are His desires too. I remember when my daughter, Becky, got her first car. We had prayed about it for a long time and knew the make and model she wanted. Finally, one evening she came to me with a news-paper in hand and showed me an ad for a car that she believed was the answer to her prayers. God had given her a promise that He would provide the right car at the right time. I wasn't so sure. Still, we made the call and after supper drove over to see it. To my amazement, it was exactly what she had asked God to give her—right down to the color, wheel covers, and price. I started to say, "Let's take some time to pray about this a little more," but God stopped me. We had prayed. We had trusted Him as a family, and now we were standing and looking at His answer. There was no way I could walk away. Becky had learned a tremendous lesson of faith. She had asked God to reveal His will, confirm it to her in His Word, and then answer her prayers. He had done His part, and now He was calling on me to do mine by hammering out a deal with the owner. You and I will never go wrong by trusting and obeying God.

You may be praying and asking God to work in your life and situation. Maybe there is something you long to have or something you want to experience. For example, many young women pray for God to send the right man for them to marry. When they meet someone, they need to ask questions to be sure that this is God's provision for their lives. He promises to meet every need you have. But you want to make sure that you are getting His best and are in step with His will. I cannot begin to write of the times that I have heard people say, "I thought he was the perfect one." Or "She fit every desire I had for a wife." After the marriage papers are signed and the guests have gone home, two people are left alone to sort through a huge amount of changes, adjustments, and feelings. At this point, you want to know, without a doubt, that you have received God's very best.

When you trust God for promises in His Word and feel as though He has answered, ask yourself the following questions about your choice.

Does this promise meet my personal need or desire? Sometimes we can want something so badly that we make choices without considering the consequences. But if we wait for God and remain committed to be right in step with His will, we will receive His blessing, and it will be more than we imagined. In fact, it will be the best. We may be right on target and have chosen the right course of action. If this is the case, then God promises that we will hear His voice or at least sense His leading telling us that this is the right way (Isa. 30:21).

Have I submitted my desires to His will? This is a crucial step. I once knew a woman who wanted to marry a man whom she had known for years. It seemed like a perfect match, but I counseled her to get alone with God and remind Him of His promises to her and ask Him if this union was His best. I also encouraged her to give the entire relationship to the Lord. "If it is God's gift to you, He will make sure you keep it. If it is not, you do not want it." I could tell by the look in her eyes that she really did not want to submit her desires to God. She wanted to be married and was in love. That night, however, she got down on her knees and gave

God the relationship. She told Him that she was in love and wanted to marry this man, but because she loved Him more, she was offering the relationship to Him for His approval.

Three weeks later she found out that he was seeing someone else and was trying to decide which woman would best suit his personal needs. She quickly saw how God was protecting her from making a wrong mistake. Though it took a long time for her to get over the incident, she is now happily married to a wonderful guy who loves her without hesitation. God had something better in mind. She thought she had His promise, but she really had her desire and was trying to make it God's desire too. Before you make a horrendous mistake, stop and submit your life and situation to Him. You will be very glad you did.

If God answers this promise, will He be glorified? Often people are more concerned about having their needs met than they are about pleasing God. They forget that if their lives are not in step with His will, then there will be heartache, disappointment, and sorrow. However, if He is our first concern, then the decisions we make will glorify Him and He will be honored. When He is, then others will see His work in our lives and they will want to develop a personal relationship with Him.

Can God fulfill this promise to me without harming or hurting someone else and without interfering with His will for his or her life? Many times, our requests are "me" centered. We want things that are not necessarily bad, but they may be things that could draw someone else away from the Lord. You cannot just pick a promise out of His Word and claim it as your own or push to achieve it in your life. God has a plan, and He always takes into account your life and the lives of others around you. Therefore you need to pray, "Lord, this is what I want to do, but I want to make sure that it lines up with Your will for my life and that it will not harm anyone else." God's promises given always bring blessing and hope. They never subtract or take away our emotional strength or faith; they always add and multiply what He has so generously given.

Does the Holy Spirit bear witness to my spirit that God is pleased with this promise? You may want something so desperately that you will go to God's Word, choose a promise, claim it, and then tell others, "This is what God is going to do for me." But He never does. Each time you remind Him of what you have read in His Word, you sense His quietness of Spirit. He is waiting for you to get in line with His will and stop trying to make something happen that is not His best for your life. One woman told me that when she accepted a job in another city she went through a period when she felt very lonely. Each night before going to bed, she looked up Scripture verses about friendship and prayed them back to the Lord. She was a long way from home and a long way from her family and friends. Surely God wanted her to have a friend—someone she could at least talk over the events of the day with.

Weeks rolled by, and while she met a few people, no one really "clicked" with her. Finally she decided that she would find a friend on her own. The Bible talked about friendship, God knew it was not good for a person to be lonely, and she had had enough! Weeks later she ended up on her knees confessing that she had made some very wrong choices. She realized that she should have waited for God's gift of friendship, but she had forged ahead and ended up being in the company of people who did not know Him or love Him the way she did. The wondrous thing about God is that He stands ready to forgive and restore the moment we acknowledge our sin and need for Him. He redirected her life and provided godly fellowship for her. As we talked at length, I believe she also came to an even greater understanding about God. He had allowed her to go through this time of loneliness because He wanted to draw her closer to Himself. In no way was He seeking to harm or discourage her. He only has the best in mind for our lives, and that always begins with an intimate relationship with Him.

By claiming this promise, am I contradicting God's Word in any way? You always want to make sure that what you are asking God to do is in alignment with His will for your life. It also needs to be something that is biblically on target. Solomon prayed for wisdom, and this was exactly what he needed and what God had planned to give him. When we study God's Word, we are going to begin to think like He does. As we consider the context of our lives and the goals we want to reach, God will give us promises in His Word that we can claim for encouragement. When we seek God, we will gain His mind about our situation. He may not remove our trials, but He will give us such a strong sense of hope that we will be able to endure to the end with a spirit of victory and reward. God wants us to claim His promises, not just to gain a material blessing, but so that we can understand His truth for our lives. A promise made to us by God emphasizes His greatness, His faithfulness, and His unchanging love for us. In other words, when we know that we are in step with God's Word, we can say, "God said it and that settles it."

If God answers this promise, will it further my spiritual growth? The answer to this question should be a flat-out "Yes!" If you have to think about it or try to convince yourself that gaining the answer to your promise will actually be good, then either you have missed the point, or you are off track with God. He tells us to trust Him, acknowledge His faithfulness, and not to be wise in our own eyes. When we do trust Him, He promises to make our paths straight. In other words, we will know the way to go and the right decision to make because God's Spirit has promised to guide us and we have the truth of His Word to back it all up. We no longer try to "slip" something by God. Our arms are open, our knees are bent, and our faces are turned toward Him. We have submitted our hearts and lives to Him, and in return we have been given an overwhelming sense of peace along with His assurance that whatever we need, He will provide it and so much more (Phil. 4:19). How could we deny Him the opportunity to bless us in this way?

By now you probably realize that claiming a promise of God is not a simple matter. It takes faith, obedience, and patience. But even more than these three, gaining the promises of God requires a deep abiding love for Him. Trust, obedience, and a willingness to wait for God to fulfill His promises to you come as a result of the overflow of our unbridled love for the Savior. If you have never given your life to Christ—I'm not talking about salvation—I'm talking about laying your life down and taking up His life as your own—then you cannot fully experience the joy that comes from claiming His promises by faith and watching Him fulfill each one. Your heart will be divided between what you want to do according to the world's standard and what God says is right. Living the Christian life comes down to one question: whom are you going to serve, Jesus or yourself? When you make a commitment to serve the Savior, your life will change. Suddenly there will be so many promises you can claim that you will not know where to begin. And the blessings will be endless. You don't have to make the same mistake that others have made. You can choose to trust Him, to commit your way to Him, and to delight in His precepts, and you will be able to claim His promises for yourself, your children, your spouse, your business, and your friends. And you will quickly discover that the goodness God has for you will never end.

CHAPTER 8

TRUST GOD AND OBEY HIM

The most important lesson we can learn as believers is to trust God. Nothing else compares with this—nothing comes close. When you know you are doing what God has called you to do, there is a sense of security and surety surrounding your life that is obvious to others. Decisions, while they may seem tough, are made effectively because your mind and heart are focused not on what you want to do but on what God wants. There is a huge difference. When we push to gain an answer to our prayers or to have something we feel we need, there is always a feeling of uneasiness within us. It should never be hard to trust the Lord because His love for us is so great. However, unless we know for sure that we are walking in step with Him, we will constantly think, *Lord, am I doing the right thing? Did I make the right decision? Are You okay with what I'm doing?* I'm not talking about asking Him to affirm you. God wants and even listens expectantly for us to pray asking Him to draw us close to His heart. "O

Lord, You have heard the desire of the humble; You will strengthen their heart, You will incline Your ear" (Ps. 10:17). God hears our prayers. He knows all about the silent cries of our hearts, but He also knows our joys. We can trust Him fully because He knows all about us and loves us unconditionally.

Why Elijah Ran

When it comes to trusting God unconditionally, there are several people in the Bible whom we could list as examples—Moses, David, Joseph, Isaiah, Jeremiah, all of the minor prophets, and many in the New Testament. While there were times when they demonstrated great faith, there were also moments when their faith and trust in God waned. Moses became angry with the people and hit the rock with his staff to bring forth water for them to drink. David made a horrendous decision when he chose to count Israel's fighting men—those who could go into battle. The prophet Elijah stood on Mount Carmel and defeated every one of the prophets of Baal. Yet hours later he was on the run in fear of losing his life at the hands of a wicked queen. Four hundred and fifty false prophets could not accomplish what one angry woman was able to do—frighten God's messenger to the point of running away from where God had placed him. When does strong faith—immovable faith—turn into fear? The answer is easy: when we take our eyes off of the Source of our strength and place them on our circumstances, personal desires, or things that we know are not God's best.

Anytime we pause to consider a way other than God's way, we run the risk of becoming frustrated. There was no reason for Elijah to become besieged with fear. God had gained a great victory, and His prophet was at the hub of the activity. However, this did not stop the enemy from harassing him with thoughts of death and fear. Instead of going out to meet Jezebel, he headed off in the opposite direction and ended up hiding out in a cave explaining to God how he arrived at this distressing point. "I have been very zealous for the LORD, the God of hosts; for the sons of Israel have forsaken Your covenant, torn down Your altars and killed Your prophets with the sword. And I alone am left; and they seek my life, to take it away" (1 Kings 19:10). Can you imagine these words coming from God's prophet—a man of such tremendous faith that he boldly challenged several hundred false prophets, saying, "Call on the name of your god. . . . Call out with a loud voice, for he is a god; either he is occupied or gone aside, or is on a journey, or perhaps he is asleep and needs to be awakened" (18:25, 27)? There was no answer from Baal because there is only one God and that is the Living God, the God of the Bible, the God who loves us and has saved us with His mighty outstretched hand.

I love what God said to Elijah as he was hiding in the cave. He did not acknowledge His servant's lack of faith. It was obvious that Elijah was in a narrow place—emotionally, spiritually, and physically. He was frightened. He didn't think he could go back because he was sure that he would be killed. And he did not know how he would go forward, but God knew exactly what He would do to refresh, renew, and restore the faith of His prophet. The Lord commanded Elijah:

> "Go forth and stand on the mountain before the LORD." And behold, the LORD was passing by! And a great and strong wind was rending the mountains and breaking in pieces the rocks before the LORD; but the LORD was not in the wind. And after the wind an earthquake, but the LORD was not in the earthquake. After the earthquake a fire, but the LORD was not in the fire; and after the fire a sound of a gentle blowing. When Elijah heard it, he wrapped his face in his mantle and went out and stood in the entrance of the cave. And behold, a voice came to him and said, "What are you doing here, Elijah?" (19:11–13)

God did not have to announce His coming. All of nature brims with the awareness of who He is. His coming was so great and mighty that the mountains were torn and shaken by His presence. He could have leveled the earth surrounding the prophet, but a display of His omnipotence was not His intent. It was the gentle whisper that humbled Elijah and reminded him whom he served. Even though he recounted his story to God, the Lord did not acknowledge it. He had moved way beyond the point of citing an evil queen for the wrong she had done. He knew her end. He was more interested in getting His prophet back on track. "The LORD said to him, 'Go, return on your way to the wilderness of Damascus'" (19:15).

God sent His prophet back into the heat of the battle, and He often does the same thing with us. Even though Elijah had assumed the moment he left his base camp on Mount Carmel all was over, God had a different plan. His faithfulness has nothing to do with our circumstances. Elijah, like we may do, lost sight of this. Fear struck a chord in his heart, and suddenly his courageous spirit and well-trained faith evaporated. But notice what God did not do. He did not major on Elijah's weaknesses. He did not chasten him for becoming weak under pressure and when threatened by the enemy. Instead, He ordered him back to the place that he had left. There he would begin a new work—one that would lead to an even greater ministry and one that would be passed on to a young prophet named Elisha. In doing this, God gave His prophet a refresher course on His greatness, faithfulness, power, and infinite wisdom. The scene is reminiscent of what the psalmist wrote in Psalm 18:

> He rode upon a cherub and flew; and He sped upon the wings of the wind. He made darkness His hiding place, His canopy around Him, darkness of waters, thick clouds of the skies. From the brightness before Him passed His thick clouds, hailstones and coals of fire. The LORD also thundered in the

heavens, and the Most High uttered His voice, hailstones and coals of fire. He sent out His arrows, and scattered them, and lightning flashes in abundance, and routed them. Then the channels of water appeared, and the foundations of the world were laid bare at Your rebuke, O LORD, at the blast of the breath of Your nostrils.

He sent from on high, He took me; He drew me out of many waters. He delivered me from my strong enemy, and from these who hated me, for they were too mighty for me. (vv. 10–17)

We may think that our enemies, whether real or imagined, are too great for us, but they are not for God. He is over all things. And we can trust Him because He is trustworthy—this is His nature, His character, and one of His many attributes.

A GOD WHO NEVER FAILS

Elijah needed to be reminded of God's power, strength, mercy, and grace. And most of all, he needed to recall the faithfulness of God. The Lord never abandons us. When He calls us to do a certain task, He will give us the ability and the means to get it done. I can imagine that Elijah's trip back to Damascus was a lot more eventful than the one he had taken earlier. On his return, he carried with him the memory of being in God's omnipotent presence. No matter how frightening that may have seemed, it certainly quenched the flame of fear that threatened to destroy his work and testimony as a prophet of God. Can you recall a time in your life when God broke into your out-of-control emotions with such power and majesty that you were completely stopped in your tracks? Most of us can list one or two times. Elijah did not offer another excuse as to why he had left his post. He gathered up his things and went back the way he had come. Only this time, the journey he took reshaped his life.

As we study God's Word, it is very important to understand that He does not change. The events and circumstances that frighten and threaten to alter our lives do not change or alter Him. He is infinite, unshakable, faithful, true, trustworthy, all-loving, all-knowing, and all-powerful. Regardless of the packaging wrapped around today's idols, one thing remains true: God is sovereign over all things. He has allowed us to have so much, but many times the very things that have been created with the thought of streamlining our workloads have actually added confusion, dissatisfaction, and anxiety to our pace. We can become so consumed thinking about whether to take our laptop computers on vacation that we don't have time to stop and think of the goodness of God's blessing to us. Another thing I have noticed is that when we insist on keeping our cell phones and computers within arm's reach, we rarely relax and enjoy what God has given us. We are still hooked up to the world's system. Why should we think about trusting Him? Help or conversation with a friend, coworker, or peer is only a dial tone away or waiting for us with the click of a "send" button.

Elijah did not have to run, but he did. His spiritual eyes grew dim temporarily. Like Peter during the storm on the Sea of Galilee, his focus shifted from Jesus to the earthly elements around him, and he was frightened. We sing the following words from the hymn "Trust and Obey," but do we believe what we are singing? *When we walk with the Lord in the light of His Word, what a glory He sheds on our way! While we do His good will, He abides with us still, and with all who will trust and obey. Trust and obey, for there's no other way to be happy in Jesus, but to trust and obey.*

God immediately dealt with the fear in these men's lives. He knew if they continued along this path, they would never be prepared for what He had next for them. How do you handle fear—the ultimate barrier to faith? There is only one way and that is through faith in God and by walking in the light of His Word. The Bible is our textbook on faith, trust, and obedience when it comes to God. It also provides foundational principles that teach us how to live godly lives so that we experience His blessings, goodness, and protection even when life takes a sudden turn in a direction that we do not want to travel.

No one wants to receive the news that his or her loved one is gravely ill or has tragically passed away. However, when your faith is founded in Christ, you will not be easily shaken. Momentarily Elijah ran and Peter cried out, and each one of us has done the same thing at some point. Jesus said, "All that the Father gives Me will come to Me, and the one who comes to Me I will certainly not cast out" (John 6:37). You do not have to fret or worry about whether He will always love you. The answer is yes. No matter what you have done or will do in the future, God's love for you remains true. Therefore you do not have to be anxious about tomorrow. Jesus instructed His disciples to keep their eyes focused on one thing—the very thing that mattered the most and that was God. "Seek first His kingdom and His righteousness, and all these things will be added to you. So do not worry about tomorrow; for tomorrow will care for itself. Each day has enough trouble of its own" (Matt. 6:33–34). Fretting about the future and about things that probably will never take place erodes your faith in God quicker than almost anything you can do.

When I was young, my mother had to work two jobs to pay our monthly bills. There were times when I worried if we would make it. I'm sure she thought the same thing, but she never voiced this concern. Instead, she prayed every night for God to take care of our needs and to allow us to have enough left over at the end of every month just in case we had an emergency or needed to help someone else. God never failed to provide for us. I grew to look at this time in my life as a season of extreme blessing. God taught me more about His faithfulness in those lean years than in all the years that I read and studied in college. I was in God's classroom. I was His private student, and He was tutoring me in the subjects of faith, trust, and obedience. These are interlinked and cannot be separated. If you learn to trust God, you will have great faith—perfect faith in Him—and you will obey Him regardless of all else.

He Rewards Those Who Trust

Over the years I have talked with missionaries who are serving overseas and heard how difficult life on the mission field can be. Satan is relentless in his pursuit of those God has placed in areas where the gospel is not welcomed or embraced by country leaders. There are underground churches in countries like China and North Korea that are growing and vibrant. Yet the work of the missionaries can be exhausting, and every step they take, the enemy takes with them—belittling their efforts, tempting them to think that they are forgotten, and coaxing them to give up. I tell my friends who are overseas, "Stay focused on what God has given you to do. Trust Him. He has not and never will forget you. Remain true to the call and know that He will provide all you need to accomplish every single task." You do not have the privilege of walking out on the will of God. No matter how hard life becomes, God knows when it is time for you to move and when it is time for you to remain. If your trust and faith are in Him, you will be able to endure and one day receive the blessings that He has for you—just as Joseph did in Genesis 41:39–42: "Pharoah said to Joseph, ' . . . You shall be over my house, and according to your command all my people shall do homage; only in the throne I will be greater than you . . . See, I have set you over all the land of Egypt.' Then Pharaoh took off his signet ring from his hand and put it on Joseph's hand, and clothed him in garments of fine linen and put the gold necklace around his neck."

Psalm 37 instructs us not to worry. Worry and faith do not mix—they are like oil and water. We cannot trust God and fret about what is going on in our lives or what will happen in the future. This does not mean that we are to act unconcerned. But it does mean we are to stop rushing from one person to another seeking advice and listening to the opinions of others without taking time to hear what God has to say. We need to stop, drop to our knees in prayer, and roll the burdens of our hearts over onto Him. He is the only One who can solve every problem we face. The psalmist wrote, "Do not fret because of evildoers, be not envious toward wrongdoers. For they will wither quickly like the grass and fade like the green herb. Trust in the LORD and do good; dwell in the land and cultivate faithfulness. Delight yourself in the LORD; and He will give you the desires of your heart. Commit your way to the LORD, trust also in Him, and He will do it. He will bring forth your righteousness as the light and your judgment as the noonday. Rest in the LORD and wait patiently for Him" (Ps. 37:1–7).

Do not fret. Don't worry because God is trustworthy. He

never fails to keep His promises. Circumstances may turn dark and stormy, but the same God who stood up in the boat on the Sea of Galilee and commanded the raging wind and the bellowing waves to be still stands watch over your life.

Trust in the Lord. Allow Him to have complete control of all that concerns you. People often fight to stay one step ahead of God. One woman told me that she paid every single bill that was mailed to her on the day of its arrival. In other words, she opened her mail and then sat down and wrote out a check and mailed it. Her reason for doing this was not what you would expect. She was afraid that should something happen to her, her bills would not be paid on time. A part of this is admirable, especially in a day and time when many people disregard their bills altogether. However, it was maddening for her to rush to get something back in the mail so quickly. She could not relax until the bill was paid. God wants us to trust Him, to allow Him the privilege of being our heavenly Father who knows all about us and faithfully provides what we need when we need it.

Delight yourself in the Lord. When your faith is sewed up in Jesus Christ, you can enjoy yourself and not have a sense of uneasiness hanging over your heart. People who have never truly learned to trust God always feel just a little bit anxious. They know He is God, they have asked His Son to be their Savior, but they have never relaxed and taken hold of His mighty hand. They are still hanging on to the things they believe will bring security.

He gives you the desires of your heart. God wants us to trust Him—to find delight in His presence. When we do, He gives us the desires of our hearts. It is His will, purpose, and plan to give us good things. He knows what we need, but more than this, He knows what we like and want. When our lives are caught up in Him, we will want the things that honor Him, and they will also be the very things that bring us the most joy. After all, who gives us desires? God is the One who prompts us to want certain things. One college student asked, "You mean God doesn't mind me having a car of my own?" Absolutely not! He gives good things to His children, but we must ask Him for the things we desire. And when we do, we need to have the right motive, which is one that is in step with His will for our lives.

Commit your way to Him. The psalmist instructs us to roll our way over onto God. The older saints often talked about rolling their burdens onto God because He is our burden bearer. In Psalm 55:22, the psalmist writes, "Cast your burden upon the LORD and He will sustain you; He will never allow the righteous to be shaken." This is the same concept except we are giving our future to Him. We relinquish our need to direct our own course. Instead, we ask Him to make the way before us clear and we follow where He leads. I have had people tell me that they are "trusting God," but the entire time they are talking, you can feel the wheels turning as they plot their next course of action.

"Commit your way to Him" means letting Him have all that concerns you. You will stand ready for His instruction and won't fret about what you need to do next because you have learned that when it is time to move or change direction, He will make this clear to you.

Trust Him because He is faithful. God knows our weaknesses and how easily we are drawn off course. God had not scheduled a detour for Elijah. He took off on his own, and when he had exhausted every means of escape, God appeared to him. When you and I are walking in the will of God by placing our faith in Him, it doesn't matter how great the threat may be or how dark the storm clouds become. God is with us. He is the anchor to our souls. We can stand upon the immovable rock of God Himself— unshaken—knowing that He is in control of all things. It is amazing what we can accomplish when we give Him our lives and hold nothing back.

Rest in the Lord and wait for His provision. Trust and faith lead to one end, and that is rest and peace. You cannot be anxious and rest at the same time. And you can't fret and wait with patience for His goodness to be revealed. There are some things that God gives us the ability and knowledge to fix. Other times He wants us to wait because He is preparing the way before us, and He knows that one of the best ways to reveal the level of our faith in Him is through waiting—a week, a month, and maybe in some cases, like Joseph, years. Does time determine the faithfulness of God? No, but our ability to wait for His goodness, guidance, and direction certainly does. If I'm resting in Him, I'm not arguing with Him about what needs to take place. I'm relying on God to be. I'm submitted to Him. I'm trusting Him and looking with expectation for the day when He will make His will even clearer to me.

THE REASONS WE CAN TRUST GOD

There are specific biblical reasons we can trust God.

We can trust Him because He is God. Nothing and no one is like Him. He is the only God, the sovereign God, the supreme God. And the Bible tells us that His name is Jehovah—Lord. When He sent Moses to Egypt to release the Israelites from captivity, He said, "'I AM WHO I AM'; and He said, 'Thus you shall say to the sons of Israel, 'I AM has sent me to you'" (Exod. 3:14). On the dark night of Jesus' arrest, when it appeared that Satan was in full triumph, God's power was evident. When Judas and the temple officers approached Jesus in the garden, He asked them, "'Whom do you seek?' They answered Him, 'Jesus the Nazarene.' He said to them, 'I am He.' . . . So when He said to them, 'I am He,' they drew back and fell to the ground" (John 18:4–6). You can't stand with a heart of defiance in God's presence. You might be able to stand with hands lifted up to Him in worship but with a heart bowed in reverence and honor. But I have a strong inclination that if we saw the Lord—if we stood in

His presence the way Moses did or Elijah did—we would fall on our faces in worship, praise, and complete adoration. "I AM"—the God who created the world, who spoke the heavens into being, who divided the Red Sea so Israel could walk through on dry land, and who created you and calls you beloved—is all you need to know about Him in order to trust Him with every area of your life. We think, *Well, I can trust this friend or this family member,* and maybe you can. But the God of all love and compassion, the One who has promised never to leave you, is waiting for you to trust Him.

We can trust Him because He is the very essence of truth. God cannot lie. Truth is at the very heart of the nature of God. He can only speak the truth. Therefore, when we go to Him in prayer asking for wisdom, we know we will receive it. When we need to know that we have done the right thing, acted wisely, and chosen the correct pathway, He will confirm it to us. Friends often tell us what they think we want to hear. It is easier for them to feel accepted if they believe they are well liked. But God is not concerned about our "liking" Him. He wants us to learn just how much we need Him. He won't tell us one thing and then change His mind because He knows we need truth. We may not always like what we hear. However, when we discover the consequences that come from making a wrong choice, we usually are very eager to know what is right and what we need to do. Truth speaks to the heart of the believer, but those who do not know Him despise His truth and the truth of the gospel message.

We can trust God because He is faithful. Jeremiah reminds us of this very thing: "This I recall to my mind, therefore I have hope. The LORD'S lovingkindnesses indeed never cease, for His compassions never fail. They are new every morning; great is Your faithfulness. . . . The LORD is good to those who wait for Him, to the person who seeks Him" (Lam. 3:21–23, 25). I can always trust Him no matter what. Over the years I have counseled many people who have suddenly found themselves separated after years of marriage. Regardless of what led to one spouse leaving, the astonishment is the same: "I never thought he would leave me." "She promised 'till death do us part.'" While God's goal for marriage is never separation, there is only one Person who has promised never to leave us and that is Jesus Christ. He is with us the moment we take our first breath, and He will be with us when we take our last. He also will be with us throughout all eternity. He is the only One who can say, "I will never leave you."

We can trust Him because He has promised to answer our prayers. Jesus told His followers, "Ask, and it will be given to you; seek, and you will find; knock, and it will be opened to you. For everyone who asks receives, and he who seeks finds, and to him who knocks it will be opened" (Matt. 7:7–8). The key to receiving God's promise is faith and trust in Him. If we trust Him, we will seek Him, and if we seek Him, we will find Him and also gain His blessings for our life. This is a natural overflow of obeying God by trusting Him. It is a very simple principle of life that tells us for every action, there really is a reaction. This is so easy to accept when we think of this principle from the world's perspective. But it is just as true concerning the things of God. If you trust Him, you will gain His blessing, but you also will be given so much more—more insight, wisdom, knowledge, discernment, peace, joy, contentment, hope, and faith in Him. Your faith will grow as you learn to trust Him with every detail of your life. This is because God is in the process of teaching us how to live in a relationship with Him that makes life complete, and no matter what our troubles are, He will give us an overwhelming sense of joy and peace.

We can trust Him because He is all-powerful. Nothing is greater than God. Empires have come and gone, but God remains the same. Men have written volumes of books about what they perceive to be true, but nothing has the power and potential of the Word of God. Nothing written contains more truth or has outlasted the Word of God. Evil governments have tried to annihilate it, but this will never happen. Jesus is the living Word of God, and the grave could not hold Him (John 1:1–3; 20:17). He gave His disciples all power and authority because it is exactly what the Father had given Him and this is exactly what He wants to give each one of us (Luke 10:19–22). The way you can tap into this power is through a personal, loving relationship with the Savior, which means loving Him enough to read and study His Word.

Only God has the power to make a promise and to keep it. There is not a time when He is taken off guard or by surprise. He knows what is taking place in the Middle East, but He is just as aware of the pressures building in your personal life. He is the God who cares intimately about you. Every word of Scripture has been given by Him to guide, protect, encourage, and direct you as you live your life for Him.

We can trust Him because He loves us unconditionally. There is no limitation to God's love. He never says, "I will love you if you do this." Or "If you disobey Me, I will remove My love from you." Love is not optional to God. He is love; therefore, He loves us unconditionally. He cannot deny His nature and character. When we walk in the center of His will, He loves us. When we yield to temptation and fall deeply into sin, His love for us continues. He doesn't condone our sinfulness or overlook it as some would like to believe. He is a God of love, but in loving us, He knows that this includes times of discipline. Sin has unavoidable consequences. And though He will never remove His love from those who have accepted His Son as Savior, He still allows them to suffer the penalty that comes with disobedience and rebellion against God. One man told me, "I'm not rebellious!" But I quickly pointed out that all sin is rebellion against God because it goes against the very principles and commandments that He has given us. John 14:15 says, "If you love Me, you will keep My commandments." If we truly love God, we will want to please Him more than we want to please ourselves. It will be a joy to keep His commandments by refusing to squander our lives as the prodigal did on reckless living. Once he came to his senses and realized how much his father loved him, he came home (Luke 15:11–32), and you can too, if you have wandered away from God.

HIS LOVE NEVER CHANGES

James writes, "Every good thing given and every perfect gift is from above, coming down from the Father of lights, with whom there is no variation or shifting shadow" (1:17). Where in the world would our faith be if God changed or if we had to worry whether He loves us or not? We never will. He loved us so much that He sent His Son to die for us. God is faithful. From the moment Adam and Eve sinned against Him, God put into motion a plan to redeem humanity. This was fulfilled through the life and death of His Son, the Lord Jesus Christ. It is through our faith in Him and by the marvelous work of His grace that we are saved. And God took His plan one step further; He restored what had been lost—the fellowship man once enjoyed with God the Father is available to all who draw near to Him—the God of love and the One who is forever faithful and true.

CHAPTER 9

BE FAITHFUL IN PRAYER AND
HAVE A HEART FOR WORSHIP

Do you pray with confidence and assurance knowing that God hears your prayers and will answer? Or do you hesitate and wonder what He thinks about you and all you have done? I want to assure you that the one thing that pleases God the most, outside of your coming to know His Son as Savior and Lord, is to hear your voice speaking to Him in prayer and worship. And while we don't have to motivate Him to move on our behalf, He is moved—touched and blessed—by the prayers we pray. Yet many people wonder if God hears their prayers. Past sins and failures have left them feeling guilty and unworthy to come before His throne. When you ask them if they have prayed about their need or struggle, you hear a heavy sigh. "God's not listening," one man told me. "I'm a sinner and He won't answer." He is not the only one who has said these same words to me. Others have admitted, "I feel so guilty and unworthy. How could God possibly answer my prayers? Look what I have done."

God hears every prayer we pray. When the enemy tells you that He does not, then you need to remember that he is a liar. Jesus said of Satan, "There is no truth in him. When he lies, he speaks his native language, for he is a liar and the father of lies" (John 8:44 NIV). In other words, if you hear a voice telling you that God is not listening, doesn't care, and cannot help someone like you, then you should automatically know the opposite is true. You are dearly beloved of God. He created you in love with a specific purpose, and that is for you to know and to enjoy an intimate relationship with Him. That is His number one goal. Yes, He wants us to take the gospel message to the lost, and that is a motivating force behind the Christian church, but it is not God's first desire. His first desire is to love you. His second desire is for you to love Him so much that you want to know Him and live your life for Him—above and beyond all else. One of the only ways this happens is in times of prayer. Without hesitation, I can say that the enemy will do everything possible to block your communication with the Lord. He will belittle you, denounce your love for God, and repeatedly tell you that you are not good enough for God to love. He has no problem bringing up as many past sins as needed to silence your prayers, specifically your bold prayers—the ones that you pray in faith trusting God to move on your behalf.

Prayer and praise are the two avenues through which we can honor God with our words. In prayer we worship before His throne and lay our requests at His feet. Nothing is too great for Him to handle and nothing too small or insignificant for His ears to hear. You can be sure that whatever concerns you concerns Him. Once you grasp this principle, you can imagine how angry the enemy will become. He will not easily douse the flames of his wicked and discouraging intent. Fact is, he will turn up the heat! But if Peter, James, and Paul were here to cheer you on, they would give you one set of instructions, and that is to persist in prayer. Be diligent, faithful, and determined, and you will be amazed at what God will do for you. This is because there is only one place where true victory is won and that is on your knees. I have often told my congregation that the distance between victory and defeat is about twelve to fourteen inches—or however long the distance is from your knees to the floor.

If you want to see God work mightily in your life, pray.

If you want the enemy to leave your presence, pray.

If you want to find true contentment, hope, and peace, learn to pray.

If you want to know the truth that will set you free, pray without ceasing to the loving God, who has a plan and purpose for your life.

Prayer is an active demonstration of our faith in God. Nothing says "I trust You" more than words spoken in sincere prayer to Him. In prayer we confess our need for a Savior and Someone who is greater than we are. We acknowledge our sin, but we also claim our forgiveness. In Romans, Paul writes, "For all have sinned and fall short of the glory of God, and are justified freely by his grace through the redemption that came by Christ Jesus" (3:23–24 NIV). We are saved by grace, forgiven by grace, loved unconditionally, and justified by God who stands watch over our lives.

You may not feel loved, but you are. And you may not feel like praying, but when you do, you demonstrate your faith in God. One small step in this area brings such joy and peace that you will want to take many more. David learned this principle early. As a shepherd boy before the pressures of life intensified, he developed a personal relationship with God based on faith. In his final days, the fellowship he had with the Lord was just as sweet and just as important to him. David never lost sight of his need for God. Even when he had more than he dreamed possible, he still worshiped and prayed to God, the one Person who knew all about him and loved him just the same.

Whose company do you enjoy? A person who can't wait to tell others what you have said to them? Certainly not. Or do you enjoy being with a godly friend whom you know you can trust— one who will let you express your deepest desires, regrets, and joys freely without a single thought of telling someone else what you have said? Without a doubt, we want to be with the person who will take care of our hearts and watch out for our well-being even when we are not in his or her company. Few things have the ability to bring peace to our hearts like being in the company of a friend—one who loves us and only wants the best for us. There is no greater friend than the Lord Jesus Christ. I have had many friends in my lifetime, but none can take the place of the Savior. He is your dearest friend. When you come into His presence, know that He is moved with love and compassion for you.

David was so caught up in God that he continually looked to see if he was pleasing the Lord. He wrote, "Seek the LORD and His strength; seek His face continually" (1 Chron. 16:11). Throughout his life, he prayed for God's help and wisdom. He did not just make rash decisions. He asked God to show him what he should do. Can you imagine how successful our country would be if our leaders decided to seek God's mind and heart concerning each decision they made? Or in your own life, think about the success you would have if you lived according to God's principles, praying each day for His wisdom and walking in faith. The Bible says, "David the king went in and sat before the LORD, and he said, 'Who am I, O Lord GOD, and what is my house, that You have brought me this far?'" (2 Sam. 7:18). He had an incredible passion for God. He also had a personal, intimate relationship with the Lord that fueled his faith. He knew a secret that you also can know and apply to your life—the power of prayer. It is written and expressed throughout God's Word. "Call to Me and I will answer you, and I will tell you great and mighty things, which you do not know" (Jer. 33:3). If you want to know God's mind for your life and circumstances, pray and believe that He will answer.

When you pray to God, you are saying, "I know You are over all things. You are God." Regardless of the level of your knowledge about Him, prayer above all else is the evidence of His lordship. Nothing proclaims His position of Creator of the universe as honestly and freely as prayer. "You are Lord. You are holy. I may not know what to say, but I know that when I come to You in prayer, something within me is changed. I gain a sense of confidence, peace, hope, and abundant joy because You are God and there is none above or beside You."

Nothing has the ability to change the direction of our hearts, minds, and lives the way prayer does. When you pray with an attitude of faith, you are saying, "Lord, I trust You to show me what is right." He will do just that, but then you will need to make another decision, and usually that is whether to obey or not. Years ago a young missionary couple became very confused over their call into the ministry. After talking with them, I felt as though the enemy was trying to blind them and prevent them from doing their work. "Ask God to show you exactly what you need to do, and He will do it," was my counsel to them. I told them I would pray and did. Months later I received a sweet letter from them saying that after that night when we talked, they made a commitment not to move an inch in any direction unless God made it completely clear in His

Word. They prayed each night together with open Bibles before them.

One would be reminded of a certain Scripture and pray it out loud before the Lord. Then the other would look up another passage and pray it. Discovering God's will for their lives and future became a journey of faith. Soon they became aware of the fact that they were no longer discussing and were only praying about their situation. Suddenly they were thanking God for His faithfulness to them and praising Him for His awesome care. They also began to pray for other missionaries. One evening as they opened their Bible and got down on their knees to pray, the husband looked at his wife and said, "You know, there is no place I would rather be than right where we are now." That was it: God had answered. Peace and contentment were at the core of their being. They had stopped focusing on what seemed wrong and were majoring on the fact that they were in the center of God's will and had no plans of leaving. God always answers prayer, but we must be open to hearing that answer. He may say, "Yes, move forward," as He often did with David. Or He may indicate that we need to wait. A person recently said to me, "When this happens, doesn't it mean God is saying no?" There was a time when I would say that God answers prayer in one of three ways: yes, no, or wait. Now I tell people that He answers prayer in one of two ways: yes or wait. Even if what we ask God for does not turn out the way we would like for it to, He is not saying no. He is saying, "Wait, I have something much better for you."

"But, Lord, I want to marry this man. He seems so right for me. Why are You saying no?" God is not saying no to you as much as He is saying, "Trust Me. I know what is best and this is not it. I have another person or another blessing coming your way. Will you wait for it?" This is a question that each one of us needs to ask ourselves. You may be trying to make a decision about an opportunity you have been given. It seems so right, and everything within you wants to go forward. However, deep inside you do not have a true sense of peace. You have tried to find Scriptures justifying your desire but come up empty-handed. You have even told yourself that if you go forward and you are wrong, then God will forgive you. And He will, but there are consequences to every decision we make. This is why it is so important to make wise decisions based on God's Word, and why it is crucial to pray and seek God's wisdom and guidance.

God called David a man after His own heart (Acts 13:22) because David spent time in prayer and worship, but also because he obeyed the Lord. He didn't just give lip service to God and then go his own way. He wanted to know what God expected from him so he could do it. When you love someone—when you love God—you will want to be with Him, please Him, and devote your entire life to Him. David never entered the presence of God with a laundry list of things he needed. He prayed for

God's wisdom so he would know what to do and how to live, but his first concern was to acknowledge the holiness, the awesome power, and the abiding unconditional love of God. David never said, "Lord, here I am and here are my needs."

He was sensitive to the Spirit of God and worshiped the Lord through prayer and adoration as he went through his day—when relaxing, while working, and while leaning back in the company of friends. God was the central focus of David's life. This doesn't mean that he never enjoyed the fellowship of others. It does mean that prayer was at the hub of his life—before he was the anointed king of Israel and until the day he died. The same was true of Jesus. Prayer was a cornerstone to His ministry. Time spent alone with the Father was where He gained insight for the work He had been given to do. It was in God's presence that He was refreshed and renewed. Though He was God in the flesh, He also was subject to human weaknesses. And mentally stepping aside from the pressures of life through prayer provided the break He needed in order to gain strength and fresh insight into the Father's will. The demands of this life can be overwhelming at times. Even without an emergency, the pace of most families and individuals is somewhere between "break-neck speed" and "off the radar."

Parents who work all day hurry home to pick up their children for soccer practice, music lessons, basketball or baseball games, and other events. We are a society that is quickly forgetting what it means to relax and rest. One mother who had been diagnosed with depression exclaimed, "I'm not depressed; I'm too tired to be depressed!" In many cases, the lives of parents and children are so jam-packed that there is not an extra moment. Prayer is not the first consideration, nor is it the second, third, fourth, or any other. People rush from one event to another, never taking time to be still in God's presence. Stress grows and pressure to perform increases until they are at the breaking point. And the sad thing about this is that life for the believer does not have to be this way. Many doctors are in the habit of putting a Band-Aid on the problem by suggesting anti-depression and anti-anxiety medication. Some people's lives have become so wired with fear and problems that they feel totally out of control, and in many cases they are. But nothing is outside of God's control. I'm not saying that medication is unhelpful. But I am saying that most of the problems we face can be solved on our faces before the Lord in prayer.

First, prayer teaches us to recall what God has done for us in the past. Remember Jeremiah wrote, "This I recall to my mind, therefore I have hope. The LORD's lovingkindnesses indeed never cease, for His compassions never fail. They are new every morning; great is Your faithfulness" (Lam. 3:21–23). One of the first things I learned about prayer was how to remind God of His promises to me. As a young man, one of the ways I learned to pray was by reading portions of God's Word back to Him. There would be a need in my life, and I would ask God to give me a promise in His Word that I could claim for guidance and encouragement. One of my favorites is Philippians 4:13, "I can do all things through Him who strengthens me." As I grew and learned more about God, Scriptures like this one would come to mind and a chain reaction of faith would take place. I moved from needing to know God's mind in a given area to having a promise that not only helped me define His will but also taught me how to trust Him to a greater degree.

I remember once being concerned about my grades in school, but after spending time in God's Word, I realized with His help I could do whatever He had given me to do. If I had never taken time to pray, to trust Him, and to acknowledge my need, I would have missed a tremendous blessing. Now when I encounter difficulty, I will think back over the many times God has spoken to me through His Word. I also recall His goodness, blessing, and even the times that were hard to bear when He brought discipline into my life. Each incident or event was an opportunity for me to be trained by God for His purpose. I didn't pray just to receive an answer. I prayed so that I would get to know God—His ways and His plan for my life. The psalmist cries out, "O God, we have heard with our ears, our fathers have told us the work that You did in their days, in the days of old" (44:1). Whenever the nation of Israel faced a challenge, they recalled what God had done for them in the past (Deut. 8:1). They immediately concluded that if He was faithful in the past, He would be faithful in the future.

Second, prayer teaches us how to be humble. You cannot come into God's presence with a proud heart. Like the publican, you may pray a well-versed prayer, but you will not experience the blessings that come from bowing down in His presence and honoring Him. God instructed Moses to remove his sandals. When the Angel of the Lord appeared to Joshua, he knew to bow before the Lord (Josh. 5:14). Perhaps he had heard Moses recount the moments he had spent in front of the burning bush. More than likely, the moment Joshua realized he was in God's presence, he dropped to the ground. James tells us to "submit therefore to God. Resist the devil and he will flee from you. Draw near to God and He will draw near to you. . . . Humble yourselves in the presence of the Lord, and He will exalt you" (4:7–8, 10).

I know there are people who cannot get down on their knees in prayer for physical reasons. But I believe that praying on our knees or on our faces before God brings a sense of humble adoration into the atmosphere of prayer that is totally charged with praise and worship. The disciples became so intrigued with the way Jesus prayed that they asked Him to teach them to pray. Jesus said:

> "When you pray, you are not to be like the hypocrites; for they love to stand and pray in the synagogues and on the street cor-

ners so that they may be seen by men. Truly I say to you, they have their reward in full. But you, when you pray, go into your inner room, close your door and pray to your Father who is in secret, and your Father who sees what is done in secret will reward you.

"And when you are praying, do not use meaningless repetition as the Gentiles do, for they suppose that they will be heard for their many words. . . . For your Father knows what you need before you ask Him." (Matt. 6:5–8)

When you pray, go to a place that is quiet. Humble yourself before Him because He knows all about you and loves you just the way you are. Honor Him with your words of praise, but learn to talk with Him as you would your best friend. He is our Savior, our Lord, and "a friend who sticks closer than a brother" (Prov. 18:24). If you never spend time in God's Word, you will never know the depth of God's love or the wondrous relationship He wants to have with you.

Third, prayer teaches us to trust God for the future. When our hearts are focused on Him, we will gain insight into what He wants us to know concerning the future. He also prepares us for events and circumstances that we will face ahead. I cannot count the times He has prepared me for some upcoming event. One example of this is when He was preparing me to move to Atlanta in the '70s. A sense of restlessness had begun to grow in my spirit.

I knew God was up to something but had no idea what it was. I was away from home preaching a revival when He began to show me He was going to move me. I had not been at the church I was pastoring very long—less than a year. The thought of another move was very unsettling. I loved where He had placed me. It was near the beach in Florida, which I enjoyed with my family. I began to ask God to show me when this was going to take place and reluctantly submitted to His will. The restlessness continued until one night after I had finished preaching, I went back to my room and got on my face before the Lord. I laid everything out to Him in prayer. I confessed my desire to stay where I was and not to move. However, deep inside, I knew any place other than the center of the will of God would be disastrous. He gave me a date in my mind, and I thought, *There is no way this can take place.* But it did. Sure enough, by that date, we had moved and were in our new home in Atlanta, Georgia.

Fourth, prayer creates an atmosphere for worship and praise. Isaiah writes:

> I saw the Lord sitting on a throne, lofty and exalted, with the train of His robe filling the temple. Seraphim stood above Him, each having six wings: with two he covered his face, and with two he covered his feet, and with two he flew. And one called out to another and said, "Holy, Holy, Holy, is the LORD of hosts, the whole earth is full of His glory." And the foundations of the thresholds trembled at the voice of him who

called out, while the temple was filling with smoke. Then I said, "Woe is me, for I am ruined! Because I am a man of unclean lips." (6:1–5)

The prophet Isaiah was overwhelmed by the power and might of God. The very fact that we enter into God's presence through prayer opens the door to worship and praise. The enemy hates praying people because they are his greatest threat. He will bring distraction after distraction to keep us from praying. One day I was deep in prayer and heard the telephone ringing. I thought about it for a moment and decided to answer just in case it was someone in my family who needed me. When I said hello, the person on the other end began to try to sell me something. By the time I closed the door to my prayer room, I felt as though I had allowed the enemy to distract me from enjoying God's presence and goodness. If you want your prayers to be effective, close your door, turn off your phone, and be quiet before the Lord. Rarely is a situation so crucial that you have to answer a telephone when it rings. Most things can wait a few minutes while you take time to commune with God. Only in His presence do we experience the unspeakable joy of being with Him and talking with our heavenly Father. This alone is reason enough to stand in awe of Him.

Many times people want me to provide a formula for them to know how to pray. From my perspective, there is only one way and that is the Bible way. Jesus gives us an example of the type of prayer that will not fail: "Ask, and it will be given to you; seek, and you will find; knock, and it will be opened to you. For everyone who asks receives, and he who seeks finds, and to him who knocks it will be opened" (Matt. 7:7–8). We pray with confidence knowing that the One who loves us more than any other hears us. We seek Him because we have a faith in an unshakable God—One who is alive, who conquered sin and death, and who is over all things. We knock because we know He will open the door to us. He knows us, loves us, embraces us, and wants to fellowship with us. He is aware of our tears, our frustrations, and the times we feel frightened, but He cannot calm the storm bellowing in our lives if we do not come to Him in prayer.

When we do come to Him, we find Him waiting, wanting to listen to every detail, and blessing us when we bless Him with our words that worship and honor Him. What is the one thing that prevents you from praying to God? Time? If it is, ask yourself, "Do I have enough time later on to deal with the consequences that come from a prayerless life?" Is it lack of interest or desire? Or do you struggle with shame and guilt? God will never condemn you. Satan does. He chatters endlessly, accusing, lying, and deliberating seeking to lead us astray and away from God's will. Never allow his words of discouragement to block the message of hope that God has for you through His Word. Set your heart on prevailing in prayer, and you will know the fellowship of Holy God.

CHAPTER 10

MEDITATE ON THE WORD OF GOD

Every day around the world, millions of people pick up the Bible and read it. They share with others what they have learned and the principles that they are applying to their lives. Every Sunday millions hear the Word of God being taught. Some people listen in great cathedrals, humble buildings, home churches, and even in thatch-roof structures. When you stop and think about it, the Bible is the most loved best seller of all time. God is not worried about being on a list. Over the years men have tried without success to destroy it, to stop it from being preached, and to persecute those who love it. But they have not been able to do it and they never will. Prisoners in the Nazi death camps would find a way to smuggle in a single copy of God's Word. Often it was divided up among the men or women to be read and passed on to the next person.

One day a prisoner may have read from Ephesians, but the next day only had a single page from the Psalms to read and study. Still, it was enough. And often the people who had a page from His Word would tell how they memorized the text just in case the guards came and they needed to chew it up and swallow it. They could have been executed for having a copy of God's Word in their possession, and they committed as much of it as possible to memory. Then when they were standing for hours in open areas unprotected from winter's cold, they could meditate on the Word of God and be reminded that He had not forgotten them.

LEARNING HOW TO SET THE FOCUS OF YOUR HEART ON GOD

The psalmist writes, "Your word I have treasured in my heart, that I may not sin against You. Blessed are You, O LORD; teach me Your statutes. With my lips I have told of all the ordinances of Your mouth. I have rejoiced in the way of Your testimonies, as much as in all riches. I will meditate on Your precepts and regard Your ways. I shall delight in Your statutes; I shall not forget Your word" (119:11–16). Most of us will never know what it feels like to have to hide God's Word. We have Bibles in several versions that we place beside our beds, on end tables, and any number of other places. We can get up in the middle of the night, turn on a light, and read the promises He has personally made to you and me. However, in many parts of the world, Christians cannot openly read or study their Bibles. They have to maintain great care in how they use their computers because they know that if government officials discover they are visiting Christian Web sites, they could be arrested, jailed, and executed. The one book that once was openly read in our schools can no longer be found in the classrooms. We once taught our children to read the stories of the men and women of the Bible, but this is seldom a priority today. And there was a time when fathers taught children how to memorize simple passages of Scripture—words that would offer guidance and assurance should they encounter difficulty. But today more children know about the latest popular celebrity than they do about how David killed Goliath.

The Bible tells us to "train up a child in the way he should go, even when he is old he will not depart from it" (Prov. 22:6). Parents would be extremely wise to teach the principles of God's Word to their children. Even when the child grows up and appears to be far from God, he will not forget what Mom and Dad taught him. This principle holds true for our lives as well. God is in the process of training us for His service. He is preparing us for the future. One of the surest ways to understand His ways and His personal love is by meditating on His truth. Prayer is extremely important, but apart from meditation it lacks depth.

As a young man, David meditated on the ways of God. He did not instantly know how to worship the Lord or how to serve Him. God instructed him just as He instructed Abraham, the prophets, the disciples and apostles, and us today. The Bible tells us, "In all your ways acknowledge Him, and He will make your paths straight" (Prov. 3:6). In other words, think on Him and His truth, speak His Word, and proclaim His principles—put them to the test and see how they will make a difference in your life. David prayed, "Make me know Your ways, O LORD; teach me Your paths. Lead me in Your truth and teach me, for You are the God of my salvation; for You I wait all the day" (Ps. 25:4–5). David wanted to know God's ways, and he understood that to do this, he had to meditate on His truth. There was no way he could write passages such as Psalm 23 without an intimate knowledge of who God is. "The LORD is my shepherd, I shall not want. He makes me lie down in green pastures; He leads me beside quiet waters. He restores my soul; He guides me in the paths of righteousness" (vv. 1–3). God guides us, but only as we draw near to Him and seek His face.

If you are going through a difficult time and you want to know that God is working on your behalf, open His Word and ask Him to guide you as you read and pray, and He will reveal Himself to you. Often I find that consciously or unconsciously, I will begin to think about some principle or aspect of God's nature. Maybe I have to make a decision or have a need that only He can meet. He may give me one word—just a thought—still I know that it is only a small glimpse of a much larger picture. He may say something like, "Ask." Nothing more. As I think about this word in relation to my circumstances, I also begin to consider the places in the Bible where God instructs us to ask Him to specifically meet our needs.

Even if I know the various Scriptures, I will look them up and write them on small cards that I can carry with me. If one particularly speaks to my need, I will concentrate on it—asking God if this promise applies to my life. I will open my books and study the meaning in the Greek or Hebrew so that I will have the clearest meaning of this verse. Then I commit it to memory. I meditate on it and think about how it applies to my life. I will ask God questions: "Lord, show me what You mean when You say, 'Ask.' How do You want me to ask You for the needs I have?" Through all of this, God's truth is being embedded in my heart, and the central focus of my life is shifting away from my circumstances to what God's Word has to say on the subject. As I meditate, God goes to work in my life in an amazing way, and He will do the same in your life.

How Meditation Works

Let's say for example that you may be struggling with fear. You do not know why you feel uneasy and frightened. You have claimed 2 Timothy 1:7, but you continue to feel insecure. Your grid system is overloaded with fearful thoughts even though you know that God has promised to give you hope, a future, encouragement, and a "sound mind." The key to gaining these is getting into His Word and allowing His truth to resonate within your heart and mind. When I use the word *meditation*, I am not talking about meditating the way the world does. Meditating on the truth of God's Word has nothing to do with the godless spiritualism that is being promoted today.

Meditating on Scripture helps to reprogram our negative, wrong thinking with truth. I usually suggest doing this for three weeks. I cannot tell you why or how this works. I just know that it does. If you will meditate on a Scripture that He has given you, you will notice a difference in the way you view your circumstances. Before I go to bed at night, I will take the small card with the passage of Scripture on it and read it. Then I will pray and ask God to hide it within my heart. I also will ask Him to work this truth in my life all night long while I am sleeping. You would be surprised at the seminary students who study Scripture this way. They read God's Word and memorize it before going to sleep, then throughout the night God is working the truth of those words into their subconscious. The next day, if they have to take an exam on what they have studied, it all comes flooding back to them. The principle is the same for us as we study and meditate on God's truth.

You might also pray, "Lord, I want to go to bed being reminded of the fact that You have chosen me. I'm Yours. You are my God. You are going to help me and You have promised to strengthen me; You uphold me with Your righteous right hand; and You are going to help me through whatever I am going through." You meditate on those words and read them every night carefully, applying them to your life. For the person who is struggling with fear, suddenly you realize that you are not alone. God is with you. Before long, your thinking has changed. The enemy sends a negative, defeating thought your way, and instantly you discern that this is not God's word to you. Jesus never would tell you that you're a failure or that you're not accepted.

What happens if you fail to make meditation a part of your life? You may remember certain Scriptures, but you will struggle in the heat of the battle when the enemy is attacking with one accusation after another. When He was tempted, Jesus stood on the Word of God (Luke 4). The enemy left His presence because he had no defense against God's written truth. "It is written, 'Man shall not live on bread alone'" (v. 4). Jesus was quoting Deuteronomy 8:3 (NIV), "Man does not live on bread alone but on every word that comes from the mouth of the LORD." Satan is defeated by God's Word. And when you memorize and meditate on it, you will notice a difference in your life. Plus, you are positioning yourself for a tremendous blessing.

What are the benefits of godly meditation?

An even closer relationship with Jesus Christ. When we set the course of our hearts on knowing God, we discover things we never knew about Him. We acquire a depth to our lives that cannot be gained any other way.

A sense of peace that is founded not on human knowledge but on the unshakable truth of God.

A clearer mind. Meditation actually increases our ability to recall what is true and right. Confusion is the enemy's folly, but when our minds are fixed on God's Word, we will not be blown one way today and another way tomorrow. Our paths will be straight and our courses sure because God is the one who is leading us.

A spiritual maturity that is anchored in God. Meditation helps us to grow up. As we study the Bible and apply God's principles to our lives, we suddenly put away childish things. This is exactly what the apostle Paul writes about in 1 Corinthians 13:11: "When I was a child, I used to speak like a child, think like a child, reason like a child; when I became a man, I did away with childish things." Are you ready to put away the things—the thoughts and the emotions—that have been holding you back? You can do this as you begin to pour yourself into God's Word and allow Him in turn to pour His truth into your life. Think about what you would gain: enough truth to carry you victoriously through every heartache, disappointment, and fear. He also will provide enough joy and wisdom for you to enjoy the rest of your life. Don't allow anything to hold you back from gaining God's perspective and His infinite blessing.

A tremendous sense of contentment. Since the beginning of time, men and women have tried to come up with a way to find contentment. The bottom line is this: contentment is found only in an intimate relationship with Jesus Christ. There is only one way to gain this, and it is through the study of, devotion to, and commitment to the very Person who has only your best in mind. You don't have to look around the next corner to see what is coming, what you can gain, or what you can purchase. God's love cannot be bought. It is a free gift that He offers everyone who comes to Him. If you have the Savior, you have all you need forever.